UNLOCKING YOUR AUTHENTIC SELF

A Comprehensive Guide to Living Authentically

COACH R. LASHUN WILLIAMS

Your Life Destiny, LLC
3223 Lake Avenue, #304
Wilmette, IL 60091

For permission requests, speaking inquiries, and bulk order purchase options, email info@yourlifedestiny.com

eBook ISBN: 978-1-967687-01-5
Paperback ISBN: 978-1-967687-00-8
Hardcover ISBN: 978-1-967687-02-2

LCCN: 2025906186

This book is dedicated to all those who are seeking to find their true selves, to those who are courageous enough to embark on a journey of self-discovery, and to those who believe in the boundless potential within each of us. May these pages ignite your inner spark, encourage your growth, and guide you toward a life filled with meaning, peace, and joy. You are not alone on this path. Your truth is your power.

To My Husband - Your love has been my steady ground, your belief in me an unshakable foundation upon which I've built this work. In moments when I doubted, you reminded me of who I am. You held space for my dreams, nurtured my soul with your quiet strength, and offered unwavering support through every high and low. Thank you for seeing me, loving me, and walking beside me with grace and devotion. This journey and this book would not exist without you.

To My Parents - Thank you for never asking me to shrink, and for always giving me the freedom to explore who I could become. Your encouragement to try, to stumble, and to rise again gave me the courage to seek my own truth. Because of your open hearts and patient spirits, I learned that identity is not something we find all at once, but something we are allowed to grow into. Thank you for honoring my curiosity and nurturing my wings. And thank you Mom for showing me how to put faith first against all adversities to fight even when it things look gloom. Watching you fight through your battles showed me how to fight through mine with strong faith and grace!

To My Grandmother - Though your physical presence is missed, your spirit is with me in every word, every lesson, and every step toward authenticity. The first woman who showed me what it means to live anchored in faith and truth. Your foundation in God was your compass, and through your prayers, wisdom, and quiet strength, you taught me that authenticity is not about being perfect; it's about being real, rooted, and whole. You lived with grace, spoke with discernment, and carried yourself with a divine confidence that could only come from knowing who you were in Him. You taught me that to be real is to be brave, and to live with integrity is to live with purpose. Your wisdom still whispers to me, reminding me that I am enough as I am. Thank you for showing me what it means to be whole and to lead with truth. Your legacy lives in these pages, in my purpose, and in every woman who chooses to rise into her truth. Thank you for laying the foundation. I Am… because you were. This is as much your legacy as it is mine.

CONTENTS

PREFACE

Welcome to this transformative journey of self-discovery! As you hold this book in your hands, I invite you to embark on a profound exploration of your inner world, a journey that will empower you to unlock your true potential and live a life brimming with authenticity and purpose.

In today's fast-paced world, it's easy to get caught up in the noise and lose sight of what truly matters. We often feel overwhelmed by expectations, societal pressures, and the constant pursuit of external validation. But within each of us lies a unique and powerful essence, waiting to be discovered and embraced.

Through insightful chapters, practical exercises, and actionable steps, this book will guide you through the process of self-awareness, self-acceptance, and self-love. We will explore the vital connection between your thoughts, feelings, and actions, and how to cultivate a positive mindset that empowers you to overcome challenges and create the life you desire.

This is not a passive read, but an active journey of self-exploration. I encourage you to engage with the material, reflect on your own experiences, and practice the tools and techniques offered within these pages. Embrace the process of transformation, knowing that each step you take, no matter how small, will lead you closer to the extraordinary person you were always meant to be.

INTRODUCTION

Have you ever felt like you were living someone else's life? Like there was a disconnect between who you are and what you're doing? You're not alone. Many of us find ourselves caught in a cycle of routines, obligations, and external pressures, leaving little room for self-reflection and authentic expression. We may be chasing after success, validation, or material possessions, yet feel a deep sense of unease, emptiness, or a lack of fulfillment.

This book is a beacon of hope, a guide to rediscovering your true self and creating a life that is both meaningful and joyful. It's a journey of self-discovery, a quest to unveil the hidden potential that lies dormant within you. It's a reminder that you have the power to shape your own reality, to define your own success, and to live a life that is aligned with your values and aspirations.

Over the course of these chapters, we will explore the essential elements of personal growth, including:

- **Self-Awareness:** Understanding your thoughts, feelings, beliefs, and values.
- **Positive Mindset:** Cultivating a positive outlook and challenging negative thought patterns.

- **Emotional Intelligence:** Recognizing, understanding, and managing your emotions effectively.

- **Self-Care:** Prioritizing your well-being and creating a life that nourishes you physically, mentally, and emotionally.

- **Building Strong Relationships:** Nurturing healthy connections with others and fostering genuine communication.

- **Overcoming Obstacles:** Embracing challenges as opportunities for growth and resilience.

- **Discovering Your Purpose:** Identifying your passions, values, and the unique contribution you can make to the world.

- **Unleashing Your Creativity:** Exploring your creative potential and finding outlets for self-expression.

- **Building a Successful Life:** Defining your own success, setting meaningful goals, and achieving financial independence.

- **Embracing Change:** Adapting to life's inevitable shifts and navigating uncertainty with grace and resilience.

- **The Power of Connection:** Finding your tribe, fostering community, and building meaningful relationships.

- **Mindfulness and Meditation:** Cultivating inner peace and reducing stress through mindfulness practices.

- **Embracing Your Spiritual Side:** Exploring your spiritual beliefs, values, and practices to find a deeper sense of meaning and purpose.

This book is not just a collection of information; it's a roadmap to personal transformation. It's a guide that will empower you to take control of your life, to embrace your authentic self, and to create a life that is truly your own. Are you ready to embark on this journey? Let's begin!

CHAPTER 1

THE JOURNEY BEGINS: EMBRACING YOUR AUTHENTIC SELF

The Power of Self Awareness

Imagine you're standing on the edge of a vast, uncharted territory. The air is crisp and alive with possibilities. You feel a surge of excitement and a hint of apprehension. This, my friend, is the beginning of your journey of self-discovery. It's a journey that starts with one crucial step: **understanding yourself**.

Self-awareness is the foundation upon which all personal growth is built. It's about taking the time to really **look inside** and explore the intricate tapestry of your thoughts, feelings, beliefs, and values. It's about recognizing your strengths and acknowledging your weaknesses without judgment.

Think of it like this: if you're trying to navigate a foreign land, wouldn't you want a map? A map that guides you through the twists and turns, the scenic overlooks, and the potential pitfalls. Self-awareness is your personal map, a guide to help you understand who you are and where you want to go.

But how do you embark on this journey of self-discovery? How do you begin to unveil the hidden treasures within your own heart and mind? The answer lies in the power of **self-reflection**.

The Art of Self-Reflection: Self-reflection is the cornerstone of self-awareness. It's a practice of taking a step back from the daily rush and noise to observe yourself objectively. It's about asking yourself questions, exploring your motivations, and understanding your reactions.

Here are a few ways to cultivate a practice of self-reflection:

- **Journaling:** Grab a notebook and pen, or open a digital document, and let your thoughts flow freely onto the page. Write about your experiences, your emotions, your dreams, and your fears. Journaling is a safe and private space for you to explore your inner world.

- **Meditation:** Meditation is a powerful tool for quieting the mind and connecting with your inner self. It's a practice of focusing your attention on the present moment, observing your thoughts and feelings without judgment. There are many different types of meditations, from guided meditation to mindfulness exercises.

- **Mindfulness:** Mindfulness is the practice of bringing your attention to the present moment without judgment. It's about being aware of your thoughts, feelings, and sensations without getting caught up in them. Mindfulness can be cultivated in everyday activities, like eating, walking, or listening to music.

- **Asking Reflective Questions:** Regularly ask yourself questions like: What am I grateful for? What is my current biggest challenge? How can I improve my communication? What am I most proud of? What am I struggling with? Reflecting on these questions can help you gain valuable insights into your thoughts, feelings, and motivations.

- **Seeking Feedback from Others:** Sometimes, it can be helpful to get feedback from others to gain a different perspective on yourself. Ask friends, family members, or mentors for their honest opinions. Be open to hearing their insights and consider their feedback objectively.

Identifying Your Core Values and Beliefs:

Your values are the principles that guide your actions and decisions. They are the non-negotiables, the things that are most important to you in life. Your beliefs, on the other hand, are your assumptions about yourself, the world, and how things work.

Identifying your core values and beliefs is a critical step in understanding yourself. It helps you align your actions with your priorities and build a life that feels authentic and meaningful.

Here are a few ways to uncover your core values and beliefs:

- **Reflect on Your Past:** Think about the experiences that have shaped your values and beliefs. Consider the decisions you've made, the choices you've prioritized, and the things that have brought you joy and fulfillment.

- **Consider Your Role Models:** Think about the people you admire and respect. What values and beliefs do they embody? What qualities do you admire in them?

- **Explore Your Passions:** What are you passionate about? What brings you joy and fulfillment? What activities do you lose track of time doing? Your passions often provide clues about your core values and beliefs.

- **Identify Your Triggers:** What situations, people, or events tend to push your buttons? Your triggers can reveal your deepest fears and insecurities, offering valuable insights into your beliefs and values.

- **Challenge Your Assumptions:** Once you've identified your core values and beliefs, take some time to challenge them. Are they serving you? Are they limiting you? Are they based on evidence or outdated beliefs?

The Power of Self-Awareness in Action:

Self-awareness isn't just about understanding yourself better; it's about using that understanding to **create positive changes** in your life. Once you have a clear picture of your strengths, weaknesses, values, and beliefs, you can:

- **Set Realistic Goals:** You're less likely to set unrealistic goals if you understand your limitations and capabilities. You can set goals that are challenging but achievable, and focus on making progress towards them.

- **Improve Your Communication:** Self-awareness helps you understand how your words and actions affect others. It allows you to communicate more effectively, build stronger relationships, and resolve conflicts more constructively.

- **Manage Stress and Anxiety:** By understanding your triggers and how you react to stressful situations, you can develop strategies for managing your stress and anxiety effectively.

- **Build Confidence:** When you understand your strengths and values, you gain a sense of confidence in your abilities. You are more likely to embrace challenges and take risks when you know what you stand for.

- **Live a More Authentic Life:** Self-awareness is the key to living a more authentic life. It helps you identify what is truly important to you and make choices that align with your values and beliefs. You can stop living for others' expectations and start living for your own.

The Journey Begins Within:

Embracing your authentic self is a lifelong journey, a process of ongoing exploration and growth. It's not about reaching a destination; it's about **enjoying the journey itself**. It's about learning to love and accept yourself, flaws and all, and using that understanding to build a life that feels truly fulfilling.

So, take a deep breath, my friend. Step onto this path of self-discovery with courage and curiosity. The most incredible journey begins within.

Unveiling Your True Potential

Imagine a seed buried deep within the earth, holding within it the potential to blossom into a magnificent flower. This seed, my dear friend, is your true potential, the unique set of gifts and talents that lie dormant, waiting for the right conditions to emerge. Just as the seed needs sunlight, water, and fertile soil to thrive, your potential requires exploration, nurturing, and unwavering belief to flourish.

The journey of self-discovery is like unearthing this precious seed, carefully removing the layers of doubt, fear, and limiting beliefs that have concealed it. It is a process of peeling back the layers of who you think you are to reveal the brilliance that lies within.

So, how do we unlock this hidden treasure? It all starts with self-awareness, the foundation upon which personal growth is built. It's about taking the time to look inward, to truly understand your thoughts, feelings, values, and aspirations. It's about identifying the unique tapestry of your personality, the threads that make you who you are.

There are many tools and exercises you can use to embark on this journey of self-awareness. Journaling is a powerful practice that allows you to tap into your inner world. By writing down your thoughts, feelings, and experiences, you create a space for reflection and insight. It's like having a conversation with your own soul, gaining a deeper understanding of your motivations, fears, and desires.

Another powerful tool is meditation, which cultivates a state of deep relaxation and self-awareness. It allows you to quiet the incessant chatter of your mind and connect with your inner wisdom. By focusing on your breath and observing your thoughts without judgment, you can gain clarity and insights into your true nature.

Don't be afraid to explore different forms of self-discovery. Experiment with art therapy, where you express your emotions through creative outlets. Engage in nature walks, allowing the beauty of the natural world to inspire and rejuvenate you. Immerse yourself in personal development books and podcasts, gleaning wisdom and inspiration from the experiences of others.

As you embark on this journey, be patient with yourself. It's a process of continuous exploration and growth. There will be times when you feel lost or uncertain, but remember that these moments are opportunities for learning and discovery. Embrace the journey, celebrate your wins, and never stop seeking a deeper understanding of who you are.

Remember, the key to unlocking your true potential is not about striving to be someone else. It's about embracing your authentic self, the unique and wonderful individual that you are. Embrace your strengths, acknowledge your weaknesses, and celebrate your uniqueness. It is in your individuality that your true power lies.

As you immerse yourself deeper into self-discovery, you might encounter certain aspects of yourself that you find challenging or even undesirable. This is a natural part of the process. It's important to remember that no one is perfect, and we all have areas where we can grow and evolve.

Embrace your imperfections with compassion and self-acceptance. Instead of focusing on your flaws, shift your attention to your strengths and celebrate the incredible being you are. It's through acceptance of all that you are, both the light and the shadow, that you can truly embrace your authentic self and unlock your full potential.

As you embark on this journey of self-discovery, you may encounter negative self-talk, those nagging voices in your head that try to convince you that you're not good enough or capable of achieving your dreams. This is a common challenge that we all face, but it doesn't have to define you.

The first step to overcoming negative self-talk is to recognize when it arises. Pay attention to the thoughts that run through your mind, particularly those that are critical, judgmental, or limiting. Once you identify these thoughts, challenge them. Ask yourself if they are truly true or if they are simply echoes of past experiences or insecurities.

Replace these negative thoughts with positive affirmations, statements that reinforce your strengths and capabilities. Affirmations are powerful tools that can reprogram your subconscious mind and help you cultivate a more positive and empowering inner dialogue.

For example, instead of thinking, "I'm not good enough," replace that thought with, "I am capable and worthy of success." Instead of thinking, "I'm not creative," replace that thought with, "I am a creative and imaginative person."

Remember, your thoughts shape your reality. By cultivating a positive and empowering inner dialogue, you can shift your mindset, build confidence, and unlock your true potential.

Self-acceptance is a vital step in the journey of self-discovery. It's about recognizing and embracing all aspects of your being, including your flaws and imperfections. It's about letting go of the need to be perfect and accepting yourself as you are.

Self-acceptance doesn't mean settling for mediocrity or ignoring areas where you can grow. It means acknowledging your strengths and weaknesses, celebrating your unique qualities, and treating yourself with compassion and kindness.

One of the most powerful practices for cultivating self-acceptance is self-compassion. This involves treating yourself with the same kindness and understanding that you would offer a loved one. It means acknowledging your struggles without judgment, offering yourself forgiveness, and reminding yourself that you are worthy of love and acceptance.

When you practice self-compassion, you create a safe and nurturing space for yourself to grow and evolve. You release the pressure to be perfect and allow yourself to be vulnerable and imperfect.

Remember, self-acceptance is not a destination; it's an ongoing journey. It's about continually choosing kindness and compassion for yourself, even when it feels challenging.

Another crucial aspect of self-discovery is embracing your individuality. It's about celebrating your unique talents, passions, and perspectives. It's about recognizing that you are not meant to fit into a mold or conform to societal expectations.

In a world that often pressures us to blend in, it's essential to embrace what makes you different. Your unique qualities are your greatest assets, the very things that make you special and contribute to the richness and diversity of the world.

Don't be afraid to stand out from the crowd. Embrace your quirks, your passions, and your beliefs. Let your authentic self shine through, and don't apologize for being you.

One of the most empowering steps you can take is to create your own definition of success. Instead of letting society dictate what success should look like, explore what truly matters to you. What brings you joy, fulfillment, and a sense of purpose?

Your definition of success might not align with conventional measures. It might involve pursuing your passions, making a difference in the world, or simply living a life that is authentic and true to yourself.

Embrace the freedom to create your own path and define your own success. Don't let anyone else tell you what you should be achieving or how you should be living. Trust your intuition, follow your heart, and create a life that is truly meaningful and fulfilling.

As you navigate the journey of self-discovery, it's essential to have a vision for your future. This vision is like a compass that guides you towards your goals and aspirations. It's a picture of who you want to be, what you want to achieve, and the life you want to create.

Creating a vision for your life involves imagining your future self. What does your life look like in a year, five years, or even ten years? What are you doing? Who are you with? What are you passionate about?

To create a powerful vision, use your imagination. Visualize yourself living your dreams, experiencing the joys of achieving your goals, and making a difference in the world. The more vivid your vision, the more powerful it becomes.

Your vision can evolve over time as you learn and grow. Embrace the process of refining your vision, making adjustments as necessary, and staying committed to your path.

Remember, the journey of self-discovery is an ongoing adventure. It's not a one-time event, but a continuous process of growth and transformation. Embrace the challenges, celebrate the victories, and never stop seeking a deeper understanding of your true self. The rewards of this journey will be immeasurable.

Accepting Your Imperfections

The journey of self-discovery often involves confronting our imperfections, those aspects of ourselves that we might try to hide or deny. But here's the truth: embracing our flaws is not a sign of weakness, it's a sign of strength and self-compassion. You see, the path to personal growth doesn't lead through a perfectly polished landscape; it winds its way through a beautiful, complex terrain, complete with valleys, peaks, and unexpected detours.

Imagine a sculptor working with a piece of raw stone. The beauty of the final masterpiece doesn't lie in erasing the flaws or imperfections of the stone. It lies in recognizing the inherent potential within those imperfections, shaping them into something exquisite. Similarly, our imperfections are not something to be erased, but rather aspects of ourselves that hold unique stories, experiences, and lessons.

Now, let's talk about self-compassion. Imagine you're a dear friend who's going through a difficult time. You wouldn't berate them for their mistakes or shortcomings; you'd offer them understanding, empathy, and support. Why, then, do we treat ourselves so differently?

Self-compassion means extending the same kindness, forgiveness, and understanding to ourselves that we would offer to a loved one. It's about recognizing that we are all human, prone to mistakes, and that our imperfections are part of what makes us who we are.

So, how do we cultivate self-compassion? It starts with noticing our self-critical thoughts. These are the voices in our heads that tell us we're not good enough, that we've messed up, or that we're not worthy. When those voices arise, treat them with curiosity rather than judgment. Ask yourself, "Where is this thought coming from? Is it really true? What would I say to a friend if they were thinking this?"

Remember, self-criticism is rarely helpful. It can lead to feelings of shame, guilt, and anxiety, hindering our ability to grow and thrive. Instead, shift your focus to self-acceptance and self-forgiveness. Acknowledge your flaws, but don't let them define you. Remind yourself that everyone makes mistakes, and that your imperfections don't diminish your worth.

Here's a powerful exercise to practice self-compassion:

1. **Identify a situation:** Think about a recent situation where you were self-critical. What happened? What thoughts went through your mind?

2. **Self-reflection:** Ask yourself: "If a close friend was in this situation, what would I say to them? Would I be as harsh on them as I am on myself? What kind of support would I offer?"

3. **Self-soothing:** Imagine holding your own hand, offering yourself comforting words, and reminding yourself of your strengths and resilience.

4. **Self-acceptance:** Acknowledge your imperfections and accept them as part of who you are. Remind yourself that you are worthy of love and acceptance, even with your flaws.

By embracing self-compassion, you create a foundation for personal growth. When we stop judging ourselves harshly, we free up energy and focus that can be channeled into self-improvement. This isn't about becoming perfect; it's about becoming whole, accepting ourselves with all our strengths and weaknesses, and ultimately, growing into the best versions of ourselves.

Now, let's explore the power of self-acceptance in action. Imagine a writer who's struggling with writer's block. Instead of berating themselves for not being productive, they might acknowledge that everyone experiences creative slumps, that it's okay to take a break, and that inspiration often comes when we least expect it. They might choose to go for a walk in nature, read a book, or spend time with loved ones, knowing that these activities can spark new ideas.

Or consider an entrepreneur who's facing a challenging business decision. Instead of dwelling on their past mistakes or fearing the unknown, they might remind themselves that they've overcome obstacles before, that they possess the skills and resilience to navigate this challenge, and that every decision, even a wrong one, offers valuable learning experiences.

The beauty of self-acceptance lies in its ability to release the shackles of self-criticism, allowing us to approach life with a sense of openness, curiosity, and resilience. It's about recognizing that our imperfections are not obstacles to overcome, but rather opportunities to learn, grow, and embrace the unique tapestry of our lives.

So, as you embark on this journey of self-discovery, remember that it's okay to be imperfect. In fact, it's through our imperfections that we truly come alive. Embrace them, learn from them, and use them as stepping stones on the path to becoming the best version of yourself. You are worthy, you are capable, and you are exactly where you need to be.

Embracing Your Unique Journey

Your journey of self-discovery is a unique tapestry, woven with threads of your experiences, dreams, and aspirations. It's not about fitting into a mold or chasing someone else's definition of success. It's about embracing the vibrant colors of your individuality and celebrating the unique path that unfolds before you.

Imagine a world where everyone followed the same script, where success was measured by the same yardstick. The world would be a dull, monochrome landscape, lacking the rich tapestry of individual experiences and perspectives. But fortunately, life isn't a cookie-cutter experience. You are a masterpiece, a unique blend of talents, passions, and dreams. Embrace this uniqueness, for it is the very essence of your being.

Your journey is not a race against others; it's a personal exploration, a dance with your own potential. It's about understanding your strengths and weaknesses, your values and beliefs, and finding joy in the process. It's about recognizing that you are not defined by your accomplishments or failures but by the journey itself.

Think of your life as a blank canvas, waiting to be filled with vibrant colors and meaningful strokes. Each experience, each challenge, each triumph adds to the beauty of your unique masterpiece. And as you paint, you discover new possibilities, explore uncharted territories, and express the depths of your creativity.

The world needs your unique perspective, your unique voice, your unique contribution. Don't be afraid to stand out, to be different, to embrace the quirks and imperfections that make you who you are. These are the very elements that add depth and richness to the tapestry of life.

Remember, success is not a destination but a journey. It's not about achieving external validation or conforming to societal norms. It's about living authentically, pursuing your passions, and creating a life that resonates with your soul.

As you embark on this journey of self-discovery, remember that you are not alone. You have within you the strength, the resilience, the creativity, and the love needed to create a fulfilling and meaningful life. Embrace your unique journey, celebrate your individuality, and let your authentic self shine.

Here are a few practical ways to embrace your unique journey:

- **Reflect on Your Values:** Take time to understand what is truly important to you. What are your core values? What beliefs guide your actions? These values will act as your compass, guiding you towards a life that aligns with your deepest desires.

- **Discover Your Passions:** What are you passionate about? What activities light you up? It might be a hobby, a cause, a particular skill, or simply spending time in nature. Embrace these passions, for they are the driving force behind your unique journey.

- **Create Your Own Definition of Success:** Don't let society dictate what success means to you. Define it on your own terms. What does fulfillment look like for you? What goals inspire you? When you define your own success, you create a path that aligns with your true self.

- **Embrace Your Imperfections:** Everyone has flaws, and these imperfections are part of what makes you unique. Instead of trying to hide them, embrace them. They are the stories you tell, the lessons you learn, and the experiences that shape you into the person you are today.

- **Celebrate Your Wins:** Don't underestimate the power of celebrating your achievements, no matter how small they may seem. Acknowledge your progress and give yourself credit for your efforts. This will boost your confidence and keep you motivated on your journey.

- **Be Kind to Yourself:** Self-compassion is crucial to embracing your unique journey. Forgive yourself for mistakes, treat yourself with kindness, and offer yourself the same support you would give to a loved one.

- **Embrace Change:** Life is full of unexpected twists and turns. Be open to change and embrace it as an opportunity for growth and transformation. Flexibility and adaptability are essential for navigating the ever-changing landscape of life.

Remember, the journey of self-discovery is a continuous process of exploration, growth, and evolution. It's about embracing the beauty of your individuality, celebrating your unique path, and creating a life that is true to yourself. So, take a deep breath, trust yourself, and embark on this incredible adventure!

As you continue on your journey, you will encounter challenges, setbacks, and moments of doubt. But know that you have the strength, the resilience, and the power to overcome any obstacle. Keep your vision clear, your values strong, and your heart open to the possibilities that lie ahead. And remember, you are not alone. There are countless people who have walked a similar path before you, and there are many more who are walking it with you now. Lean on your support system, connect with like-minded individuals, and share your journey with others.

This is your story, your unique masterpiece. Embrace it, celebrate it, and let your authentic self shine brightly. The world is waiting to be touched by your light.

Creating a Vision for Your Life

Imagine a world where you wake up every morning with a sense of purpose and excitement. A world where your goals are clear, your dreams are vivid, and you know exactly where you're headed. This is the power of creating a vision for your life, a blueprint for your future that guides your actions and fuels your passions.

It's like having a compass that points you in the direction of your desires. When you have a clear vision, you have a roadmap for your journey, a beacon of hope that lights up your path, and a source of motivation that propels you forward.

So, how do you create this life-altering vision? It all begins with a deep dive into yourself.

Reflecting on Your Dreams

Start by asking yourself some powerful questions: What makes your heart sing? What are you passionate about? What lights you up from the inside? These questions will help you tap into your deepest desires and aspirations.

Think about the things you've always wanted to do or experience. What are your wildest dreams? Perhaps you envision yourself traveling the world, starting your own business, writing a novel, or making a difference in the world. Let your imagination run wild and don't be afraid to dream big.

Visualizing Your Future

Once you've identified your dreams, it's time to visualize your future. Close your eyes and picture yourself living the life you desire. What does it look like? What are you doing? Who are you with?

Feel the sensations, hear the sounds, and taste the flavors of your ideal life. Let your senses come alive and create a vivid picture in your mind's eye.

This powerful act of visualization is like planting seeds in your subconscious mind. The more you visualize your dreams, the more you believe they are possible. It's like creating a mental map that guides you towards your destination.

Setting Clear Goals

A vision without goals is like a ship without a rudder, you'll be lost at sea. Goals give your vision shape and structure, making it tangible and actionable.

Think of your goals as stepping stones on your path to achieving your vision. They provide clear direction, break down your dreams into manageable pieces, and give you a sense of accomplishment as you progress.

When setting goals, remember to make them SMART:

- **Specific:** Be clear and precise about what you want to achieve.
- **Measurable:** Define how you will track your progress and know when you've reached your goal.
- **Achievable:** Set goals that are challenging but attainable, ensuring you're motivated and engaged.
- **Relevant:** Ensure your goals align with your values and vision.

- **Time-Bound:** Set a specific deadline for achieving your goal.

For example, instead of saying, "I want to be healthy," you could say, "I want to lose 10 pounds in the next three months by exercising three times a week and eating a healthy diet."

Creating a Vision Board

A vision board is a powerful visual representation of your dreams and goals. It's a physical manifestation of your vision, serving as a constant reminder of what you're working towards.

You can create a vision board by collecting images, quotes, and affirmations that represent your ideal life. You can use a corkboard, a canvas, or even a digital platform to create your board.

Place your vision board in a prominent spot where you'll see it every day. Each time you look at it, it will help you stay focused, motivated, and inspired.

The Power of Belief

Remember, the most important ingredient in creating a vision for your life is belief. You must truly believe that your dreams are possible. Doubt will only hold you back, while faith will empower you to take action.

Believe in yourself, your abilities, and your power to create the life you desire. Let your vision guide you, ignite your passion, and fuel your unwavering determination.

Embrace the Journey

Creating a vision for your life is not a one-time event but an ongoing process. As you grow and evolve, your vision may shift and change. That's perfectly normal. Embrace the journey, learn from your experiences, and allow your vision to evolve along with you.

The most fulfilling lives are those that are lived with intention and purpose. By creating a vision for your life, you take control of your destiny, tap into your true potential, and set yourself on a path to a life filled with meaning and joy. So, let your imagination soar, visualize your dreams, and embrace the journey of creating the life you truly desire.

CHAPTER 2

CULTIVATING A POSITIVE MINDSET

The Power of Thoughts

The world is a whirlwind of thoughts, constantly swirling around us like a relentless storm. These thoughts, both positive and negative, shape our emotions, influence our actions, and ultimately define our experiences. They are the invisible threads that weave the tapestry of our lives, shaping our reality in ways we may not even realize.

Imagine a vast ocean of consciousness, and within its depths, lies the swirling current of our thoughts. Some thoughts are like calm waves, gentle and soothing, while others are like raging storms, tossing us around and leaving us feeling overwhelmed. These storms, these negative thoughts, can have a profound impact on our well-being. They can cloud our judgment, steal our joy, and lead us down paths of self-doubt, anxiety, and even depression.

Think of a seed planted in fertile ground. If it is constantly bombarded with negative thoughts, it is like a harsh wind that stunts its growth, preventing it from flourishing and reaching its full potential. But if it is nurtured with positive thoughts, it is like a warm sun that encourages it to grow tall and strong, blossoming into something beautiful and vibrant.

Our thoughts are like the seeds of our emotions. When we focus on negative thoughts, we water the seeds of fear, anger, sadness, and despair. These emotions can become overwhelming, causing us to feel trapped in a cycle of negativity that is difficult to break free from.

Conversely, when we cultivate positive thoughts, we nurture the seeds of joy, love, gratitude, and hope. These emotions have the power to transform our lives, filling them with light, purpose, and resilience.

Have you ever noticed how a single negative thought can quickly spiral into a downward spiral of negativity? It's as if one bad seed has infected the entire garden, spreading its negativity to every plant around it.

For instance, if you have a presentation coming up at work and you find yourself thinking, "I'm going to mess this up," that single negative thought can trigger a cascade of anxieties. You might start doubting your abilities, worrying about what others will think, and feeling overwhelmed by the pressure.

However, if you choose to focus on positive thoughts like, "I'm well-prepared and I have valuable insights to share," you are likely to feel more confident and relaxed, enabling you to deliver a successful presentation.

The power of thoughts extends far beyond our emotions. They can even affect our physical health. Chronic negative thinking has been linked to a higher risk of developing chronic diseases like heart disease, diabetes, and even cancer.

This is because negative thoughts can trigger the release of stress hormones like cortisol, which have a negative impact on the immune system and contribute to inflammation.

On the other hand, positive thoughts have been shown to have a positive impact on our physical health. They can reduce stress levels, boost the immune system, and promote better sleep.

Imagine yourself standing at a fork in the road. One path leads to a lush garden filled with vibrant flowers and the sounds of birdsong. This represents the path of positive thinking, where you are nurtured by optimism, gratitude, and a sense of purpose.

The other path leads to a desolate wasteland, where the air is thick with negativity, fear, and despair. This represents the path of negative thinking, where you are constantly bombarded with self-doubt, anxiety, and a sense of hopelessness.

Which path will you choose?

The truth is, we all have the power to choose which path we want to walk. We can cultivate a positive mindset by becoming more aware of our thoughts and intentionally choosing to focus on the positive.

This is not about suppressing or ignoring negative thoughts, but rather about learning to recognize them, challenge them, and replace them with more helpful and empowering ones.

Imagine your thoughts like clouds in the sky. Some are dark and stormy, while others are bright and sunny. Instead of trying to get rid of the dark clouds altogether, you can simply choose to focus on the bright and sunny ones.

You can practice this by actively choosing to focus on the good things in your life, even when things are tough.

For instance, if you're feeling overwhelmed by stress, you can take a few minutes to appreciate the small things, like a warm cup of coffee, a beautiful sunset, or a kind gesture from a stranger.

Remember, every single thought you have is a choice. You have the power to choose which thoughts you want to focus on, and that power can make a world of difference in your life.

So, take a moment to reflect on the thoughts you've been carrying around with you. Are they serving you well? Are they helping you to grow and flourish?

If not, it's time to start cultivating a positive mindset, one thought at a time.

Start by becoming more aware of your thoughts.

Pay attention to the words you use to talk to yourself.

Are you constantly criticizing yourself or putting yourself down?

Are you dwelling on past mistakes or worrying about future uncertainties?

Once you become more aware of your negative thought patterns, you can begin to challenge them.

Instead of accepting negative thoughts as truth, ask yourself, "Is this really true? Is there another way to look at this situation?"

For example, if you catch yourself thinking, "I'm not good enough," challenge that thought by asking, "What evidence supports that belief? Can I think of examples where I have succeeded or achieved something I'm proud of?"

By challenging your negative thoughts, you can begin to shift your perspective and see things in a more positive light.

Another important technique for cultivating a positive mindset is to practice gratitude.

Gratitude is the act of appreciating the good things in your life, both big and small. It's about focusing on what you have rather than what you lack.

When you practice gratitude, you shift your attention away from negativity and towards the positive aspects of your life. This can have a profound impact on your mood, your outlook, and your overall well-being.

There are many ways to practice gratitude.

You can keep a gratitude journal and write down three things you are grateful for each day.

You can also practice gratitude meditation, where you sit quietly and focus on things you are thankful for.

Simple acts of kindness, like expressing appreciation to someone who has helped you or giving a compliment to a stranger, can also cultivate a sense of gratitude.

Remember, gratitude is a powerful emotion that can transform your life. When you focus on the good things, you create more space for joy, happiness, and contentment.

Finally, don't underestimate the power of affirmations.

Affirmations are positive statements that you repeat to yourself regularly to reprogram your subconscious mind for success.

When you repeat affirmations, you are essentially sending positive messages to your brain, which can help to shift your beliefs and change your behavior.

For example, if you want to build more confidence, you might repeat the affirmation, "I am confident and capable."

If you want to attract more abundance into your life, you might repeat the affirmation, "I am open to receiving abundance in all areas of my life."

Choose affirmations that resonate with you and that you believe in. Repeat them regularly, both out loud and in your mind.

Over time, affirmations can help to create a more positive and empowering internal dialogue, which can lead to positive changes in your life.

Cultivating a positive mindset is a journey, not a destination.

It requires effort, practice, and a willingness to challenge your negative thoughts and beliefs.

But the rewards are well worth the effort.

When you learn to control your thoughts, you gain control over your emotions, your actions, and ultimately, your life.

So, embrace the power of your thoughts.

Choose to focus on the positive, practice gratitude, and repeat affirmations that empower you.

You have the power to create a life filled with joy, peace, and fulfillment.

And the journey begins with a single thought.

Identifying and Challenging Negative Thoughts

Imagine a relentless inner critic constantly whispering negative thoughts in your ear, casting shadows over your self-worth and potential. These negative thought patterns can become so ingrained that they seem like an unshakeable reality. But the truth is, our thoughts are not facts; they are simply interpretations of our experiences. And just like a skilled artist can transform a blank canvas into a masterpiece, you have the power to reframe your thoughts and paint a more positive and empowering picture of your reality.

The first step in conquering negative thoughts is to become aware of them. Pay attention to your inner voice, the constant stream of thoughts that flows through your mind. Notice the patterns, the recurring themes, and the specific phrases that frequently pop up. Are you constantly telling yourself you're not good enough, not smart enough, or not worthy of happiness? Are you focusing on your mistakes and failures, magnifying their significance?

Once you begin to recognize these negative thought patterns, it's time to challenge them. Don't simply dismiss them as fleeting whims. Instead, ask yourself: "Is this thought truly accurate?" "What evidence supports this belief?" "Are there other perspectives I can consider?"

For instance, if you find yourself thinking, "I'm not good at public speaking," challenge that thought by asking yourself: "Have I ever successfully given a presentation? Have I received positive feedback on my speaking skills?" Remember, our minds often focus on the negative, overlooking the positive evidence that contradicts our negative beliefs.

The next step is to reframe your negative thoughts into positive and empowering ones. This process involves replacing those self-defeating statements with affirming and constructive ones. Instead of saying, "I'm not good at public speaking," you might reframe it as, "I am learning to become a confident and effective communicator."

Reframing negative thoughts requires a shift in perspective. It's about learning to see challenges as opportunities for growth, setbacks as stepping stones, and failures as valuable lessons. Instead of focusing on what you lack, shift your attention to what you have, your strengths, your accomplishments, and your potential.

One powerful technique for reframing negative thoughts is the "ABC Model." This model helps you understand the connection between your thoughts, feelings, and behaviors. It breaks down the process like this:

- **A (Activating Event):** This refers to the event or situation that triggers your negative thought.

- **B (Belief):** This is the negative thought or belief that arises in response to the activating event.

- **C (Consequence):** This represents the emotional and behavioral consequences of the negative thought.

For example, let's say you're giving a presentation and someone asks you a question you're not sure how to answer. This is the **activating event (A)**. Your mind might jump to a negative thought like, "I'm not prepared enough. This is embarrassing." This is your **belief (B)**. The consequence of this thought might be you feeling anxious, your voice becoming shaky, and you struggling to collect your thoughts. This is the **consequence (C)**.

By understanding the ABC model, you can begin to interrupt this cycle. Instead of letting the negative thought dominate your response, consciously challenge it. Ask yourself: "Is it really embarrassing to not know the answer? Is it a sign of weakness? Or is it simply an opportunity to learn and grow?"

By challenging the negative thought, you can shift your belief to a more positive one. Perhaps you can reframe it as: "It's okay to not know everything. I'm learning new things every day. This is a chance for me to ask for clarification and improve my understanding."

This shift in belief can dramatically impact your emotional and behavioral responses. You might feel less anxious, your voice become steadier, and you are able to think more clearly. You're now empowered to respond to the situation with confidence and grace.

Remember, you are not your thoughts. Your thoughts are simply temporary visitors in your mind. They do not define you. By becoming aware of your negative thought patterns, challenging them, and reframing them into positive and empowering ones, you can cultivate a more positive and fulfilling life.

The journey of transforming negative thoughts into positive ones is an ongoing process, but with practice and persistence, you can reshape your inner landscape and unlock your true potential for happiness and success.

The Art of Gratitude

Imagine a simple act, a daily ritual that can shift your entire perspective, transforming ordinary days into extraordinary ones. This act is gratitude, a potent force capable of enhancing happiness, well-being, and even your physical health. It's not about ignoring the challenges or hardships you face, but about choosing to focus on the good, the beautiful, the things that bring you joy and contentment.

Gratitude is like a magnifying glass, focusing your attention on the positive aspects of your life, highlighting the blessings you often take for granted. It's a reminder that amidst the whirlwind of everyday life, there are countless reasons to be thankful.

The practice of gratitude has been scientifically proven to boost happiness and improve mental health. Studies have shown that people who regularly practice gratitude experience:

- **Increased happiness and well-being:** Gratitude shifts your focus from what you lack to what you have, fostering a more positive outlook and sense of contentment.

- **Improved physical health:** Gratitude has been linked to lower blood pressure, improved sleep, and a stronger immune system.

- **Greater resilience:** By appreciating the good in your life, you build a foundation of positivity that helps you navigate challenges and setbacks more effectively.

- **Stronger relationships:** Expressing gratitude to loved ones strengthens your bonds and fosters a sense of connection and appreciation.

The Transformative Power of Gratitude

The transformative power of gratitude lies in its ability to change your mindset and perception of the world. By focusing on the positive, you cultivate a more optimistic outlook, reducing stress and anxiety. Gratitude helps you appreciate the little things, the simple joys that often go unnoticed in the hustle and bustle of everyday life.

Think about the things you are grateful for. Perhaps it's the warmth of the sun on your skin, the laughter of a loved one, the beauty of a sunset, or the simple act of being able to wake up each morning. These seemingly small things can have a profound impact on your well-being when you take the time to truly appreciate them.

Practical Exercises for Practicing Gratitude

The key to unlocking the benefits of gratitude is to make it a consistent part of your life. Here are some practical exercises you can incorporate into your daily routine:

1. **Gratitude Journal:** Dedicate a few minutes each day to writing down three things you are grateful for. It can be anything, from a delicious meal to a supportive friend to a beautiful sunrise.

2. **Gratitude Jar:** Keep a jar where you write down things you are grateful for on slips of paper. You can then periodically pull out a slip and read the reminders of all the good in your life.

3. **Gratitude Meditation:** Take a few minutes each day to sit quietly and focus on things you are grateful for. You can visualize the things you are thankful for or simply express gratitude mentally.

4. **Gratitude Walk:** While taking a walk, intentionally observe the beauty around you. Notice the colors, sounds, smells, and textures of nature. Express gratitude for these simple pleasures.

5. **Gratitude Letters:** Write a heartfelt letter expressing gratitude to someone who has made a positive impact in your life.

6. **Gratitude Affirmations:** Repeat positive affirmations related to gratitude, such as "I am grateful for all the good things in my life" or "I am thankful for my health and well-being."

Incorporating Gratitude Into Your Daily Life

You can weave gratitude into your everyday activities:

- **Start your day with gratitude:** Before you even get out of bed, take a moment to reflect on things you are grateful for.

- **Express gratitude throughout the day:** Take time to acknowledge the small things that bring you joy, whether it's a cup of coffee, a kind word from a stranger, or the sunshine on your face.

- **Practice gratitude in your relationships:** Make a conscious effort to express appreciation to your loved ones.

- **Focus on the positive:** When you find yourself dwelling on negative thoughts, intentionally shift your focus to the good things in your life.

The Ripple Effect of Gratitude

As you cultivate gratitude in your own life, you'll notice a positive ripple effect spreading outward. Your increased happiness and positivity will inspire those around you, creating a more positive and supportive environment for everyone.

Gratitude is a gift you give yourself, a simple yet profound practice that can transform your life. By making gratitude a conscious part of your daily routine, you'll cultivate a sense of joy, contentment, and fulfillment, enriching every aspect of your existence.

Building Resilience and Self Confidence

Resilience is the cornerstone of a positive mindset. It's the ability to bounce back from setbacks, adapt to challenges, and emerge stronger from adversity. Think of resilience as a muscle; the more you use it, the stronger it becomes. When you cultivate resilience, you unlock the power to navigate life's inevitable obstacles with grace and determination.

Imagine a young artist, filled with passion, who dedicates years to honing her craft. She enters art competitions, only to face rejection after rejection. Each setback could crush her spirit, making her question her talent. But instead, she chooses to see these rejections as valuable feedback, opportunities to learn and grow. She analyzes her work, seeks guidance from mentors, and relentlessly pushes herself to improve. This is resilience in action.

Developing resilience is a conscious choice. It's about recognizing your vulnerabilities and taking steps to fortify your inner strength. Here's how you can build resilience and unlock your potential:

- **Embrace Challenges as Opportunities:** When faced with a challenge, shift your perspective. Instead of seeing it as an insurmountable obstacle, view it as a chance to learn, grow, and become more resourceful. Remember, every challenge presents a learning opportunity, a chance to push your limits and discover your true potential.

- **Cultivate a Growth Mindset:** A growth mindset believes that abilities can be developed through effort, persistence, and a willingness to learn from mistakes. This mindset embraces challenges as opportunities for growth, seeing them as stepping stones on the path to success.

- **Practice Self-Compassion:** When you make mistakes or face setbacks, treat yourself with the same kindness and understanding you would extend to a loved one. Self-criticism can be crippling. Instead, embrace self-compassion. Recognize that everyone makes mistakes, and that setbacks are simply opportunities to learn and adjust course.

- **Develop Your Coping Skills:** Stress, anxiety, and negative emotions can erode resilience. It's essential to develop healthy coping mechanisms to manage these emotions. Techniques like deep breathing, mindfulness, meditation, or engaging in activities you enjoy can provide a buffer against stress and promote emotional well-being.

- **Surround Yourself with Supportive People:** Building a strong support network is crucial for resilience. Surround yourself with people who believe in you, offer encouragement, and provide a safe space for you to process challenges. Their support can help you stay motivated, focused, and grounded during difficult times.

Resilience is inextricably linked to self-confidence. When you cultivate resilience, you build a stronger sense of self-worth, knowing you have the inner strength to overcome adversity. Self-confidence is the belief in your own abilities, talents, and potential. It's the foundation for a fulfilling and meaningful life.

Here are strategies for building confidence and enhancing your sense of self-worth:

- **Identify Your Strengths:** Take time to reflect on your unique strengths and accomplishments. What are you good at? What talents do you possess? Celebrate your achievements, no matter how small they may seem. Recognizing your strengths builds confidence and reinforces your belief in your abilities.

- **Challenge Negative Self-Talk:** Our inner voice can be our greatest critic. Pay attention to the thoughts and beliefs that you hold about yourself. Are you being overly critical or putting yourself down? When negative thoughts arise, challenge them. Ask yourself: "Is this thought true? Is it helpful? Is it kind?" Replace negative self-talk with positive affirmations that reinforce your strengths and values.

- **Set Realistic Goals:** Setting goals that are aligned with your values and abilities can boost confidence. Start with small, achievable goals, gradually increasing the level of challenge as you experience success. Each accomplishment builds momentum and reinforces your belief in your ability to achieve your goals.

- **Step Outside Your Comfort Zone:** Stepping outside your comfort zone can be daunting, but it's one of the most powerful ways to build confidence. Challenge yourself to try new things, take risks, and push your boundaries. Each time you overcome a fear or challenge, you gain a sense of accomplishment and strengthen your belief in your abilities.

- **Practice Self-Care:** Self-care isn't selfish; it's essential for building confidence and resilience. Take care of your physical, emotional, and mental well-being. Get enough sleep, eat nutritious foods, exercise regularly, and engage in activities that bring you joy. When you take care of yourself, you feel better equipped to face challenges and embrace opportunities.

Building resilience and self-confidence is a continuous journey, not a destination. It's about embracing your strengths, challenging your limitations, and developing a positive mindset that empowers you to face any challenge with courage and determination. As you cultivate resilience and self-confidence, you unlock your true potential and create a life filled with purpose, joy, and fulfillment.

Embracing the Power of Affirmations

Imagine a seed planted in the fertile ground of your subconscious mind. It's a tiny seed, but it has the potential to blossom into a magnificent tree, bearing the fruit of your dreams and aspirations. This seed is an affirmation, a powerful statement that you repeat regularly to reprogram your subconscious mind for success.

Affirmations work by harnessing the power of repetition to create new neural pathways in your brain. When you consistently repeat positive affirmations, your subconscious mind begins to believe them, leading to a shift in your thoughts, beliefs, and ultimately, your actions.

Think of it like this: your subconscious mind is a powerful force, constantly working behind the scenes, shaping your experiences and influencing your choices. If you feed it negative thoughts and limiting beliefs, it will naturally produce more of the same. But when you consciously choose to nourish your subconscious mind with positive affirmations, you start to rewire your brain for success, leading to a more positive and fulfilling life.

Now, let's explore the practical application of affirmations. You can create your own affirmations, tailoring them to your specific goals and aspirations. Here's a simple formula to guide you:

"I am [positive affirmation] and I am [positive affirmation]."

For instance, if you're seeking greater confidence, you might use the affirmation: **"I am confident and I am capable."**

Here are some examples of affirmations for different areas of life:

For Self-Love and Acceptance:

"I love and accept myself unconditionally."
"I am worthy of happiness and success."
"I am grateful for my unique gifts and talents."
"I am beautiful inside and out."
"I am perfect just as I am."

For Success and Abundance:

"I am a magnet for success."
"I am financially abundant."
"I attract opportunities that align with my goals."
"I am achieving my goals with ease and grace."
"I am living a life of abundance."

For Health and Well-being:

"I am healthy, strong, and vibrant."
"My body is a temple, and I treat it with love and respect."
"I am radiating health and vitality."
"I have the power to heal myself."
"I am filled with energy and vitality."

For Relationships:

"I attract loving and supportive relationships."
"I communicate with clarity and compassion."
"I am surrounded by people who appreciate and respect me."
"I am a source of love and joy for others."
"My relationships are filled with harmony and understanding."

For Creativity and Innovation:

"I am a creative genius."
"I am open to new ideas and inspiration."
"I am constantly learning and growing."
"I am a master of my craft."
"I bring my unique talents to the world."

For Peace and Serenity:

"I am calm, peaceful, and centered."
"I am at peace with myself and the world around me."
"I am surrounded by love and light."
"I am grateful for the peace and serenity in my life."
"I am living in harmony with the universe."

How to Use Affirmations Effectively:

- **Choose affirmations that resonate with you.** The best affirmations are those that feel authentic and uplifting.

- **Write your affirmations down.** Writing them down reinforces the message and makes it easier to remember.

- **Repeat your affirmations daily.** Consistency is key. Aim to repeat your affirmations at least twice a day, and more often if possible.

- **Visualize your desired outcomes.** As you repeat your affirmations, imagine yourself already achieving your goals.
- **Feel the emotions associated with your affirmations.** Allow yourself to experience the feelings of joy, confidence, and peace that your affirmations evoke.
- **Remember, the key to the power of affirmations lies in your belief.** The more you believe in your affirmations, the more likely they are to manifest in your life. So, embrace this simple yet powerful technique and begin to reprogram your subconscious mind for success, love, and happiness.

As you repeat your affirmations with conviction, you'll notice a shift in your thoughts, beliefs, and actions. You'll find yourself taking steps towards your goals with renewed confidence, attracting opportunities into your life, and experiencing greater joy and fulfillment. It's a journey of transformation that begins within, so believe in yourself, embrace the power of affirmations, and watch your dreams come true.

CHAPTER 3

MASTERING YOUR EMOTIONS

Understanding Your Emotional Landscape

Imagine yourself standing on a vast, rolling landscape, a tapestry of emotions woven together. This landscape is your inner world, a constant ebb and flow of feelings that shape your thoughts, influence your actions, and ultimately, define your experience of life.

This journey of self-discovery begins with understanding this emotional landscape, recognizing the diverse array of emotions that inhabit our inner world. We often experience a whirlwind of emotions – joy and sadness, fear and anger, excitement and disappointment – each one a powerful force that can either propel us forward or hold us back.

Think of emotions as the weather patterns of your inner world. Just as sunshine brings warmth and clarity, joy can illuminate our path, fueling our creativity and enthusiasm. On the other hand, just as a storm cloud can bring darkness and disruption, anger can cloud our judgment and lead to impulsive reactions.

The key to mastering our emotions lies in recognizing their power and learning to navigate their influence. This is where emotional intelligence comes into play.

Emotional intelligence is the ability to understand and manage our own emotions while also recognizing and responding to the emotions of others. It's a powerful skill that can enhance our relationships, boost our productivity, and elevate our overall well-being.

At the core of emotional intelligence lies self-awareness, the ability to recognize and understand our own emotions in the moment. This is like having a weatherman inside us, constantly monitoring the shifts in our internal climate.

Developing self-awareness is an ongoing process that requires conscious effort and attention. It involves becoming attuned to our physical sensations, thoughts, and behaviors as they relate to our emotions.

Here are some practices that can help you cultivate greater self-awareness:

- **Pay attention to your body:** Notice your physical sensations, such as a tightness in your chest, butterflies in your stomach, or a furrowed brow. These are often early signs of emotional shifts.

- **Observe your thoughts:** Be mindful of the thoughts that run through your mind. Are they positive and encouraging, or are they negative and self-critical? Recognizing these thought patterns can provide valuable insights into your emotions.

- **Reflect on your behavior:** Notice how you act when you're experiencing different emotions. Do you withdraw when you're feeling anxious, or lash out when you're feeling angry? Becoming aware of your behavioral patterns can help you understand your emotional triggers and develop healthier responses.

Imagine a time when you were feeling particularly overwhelmed or stressed. Take a moment to reflect on your experience. What were you thinking? How did your body feel? How did you react? By examining these aspects of your experience, you can gain a deeper understanding of your emotional landscape.

As you embark on this journey of emotional self-awareness, remember that there is no judgment or right or wrong. The goal is simply to gain a greater understanding of your inner world and how it influences your life.

The journey of emotional intelligence is not a destination, but a continuous process of learning, growth, and self-discovery. It's about embracing the full spectrum of human emotions, recognizing their power, and developing the skills to manage them effectively.

Here are some additional insights that can enhance your understanding of your emotional landscape:

- **The Five Basic Emotions:** Psychologists often identify five basic emotions that are universally experienced: happiness, sadness, anger, fear, and disgust. These emotions are often experienced in combination, creating a complex tapestry of feelings.

- **Secondary Emotions:** Secondary emotions are complex blends of basic emotions, often influenced by our cultural and social background. Examples include: guilt, shame, envy, jealousy, and embarrassment.

- **The Power of Emotions:** Emotions are powerful motivators that drive our behavior and decision-making. They can influence our perceptions, impact our relationships, and shape our experiences of the world.

- **Emotions are not inherently good or bad:** Emotions are simply information, providing us with valuable clues about our needs and desires. It's how we respond to our emotions that ultimately matters.

By understanding your emotional landscape, you gain the power to navigate your inner world more effectively. You become more aware of your triggers, better equipped to manage your responses, and empowered to create a life that is more fulfilling and authentic.

Think of emotional intelligence as a superpower, enabling you to navigate the complexities of life with greater clarity, resilience, and compassion.

Managing Stress and Anxiety

In the previous chapter, we explored the vast landscape of our emotions, gaining a deeper understanding of their influence on our thoughts and behaviors. Now, we explore the realm of stress and anxiety, two unwelcome companions that can often cloud our judgment and hinder our well-being.

But fear not, for you are not alone in this journey. Millions of people grapple with stress and anxiety in today's fast-paced world. The good news is that mastering your emotions, especially managing these two powerful forces, is a skill that can be cultivated with time, patience, and the right strategies.

Imagine a serene lake, its surface undisturbed by the gentle breeze. This is the state of mind we strive to achieve when confronting stress and anxiety. It's not about eliminating them entirely – those emotions serve important functions in our lives. They can be signals, urging us to take action or adapt to challenging situations. However, it's about learning to navigate them effectively so they don't overwhelm us.

So, how do we achieve that inner calm?

The Power of Mindfulness

Mindfulness is like a beacon, illuminating the present moment without judgment. It allows us to step back from our racing thoughts and observe them without getting swept away. This practice, often associated with meditation, is not a passive exercise; it's an active engagement with our experiences.

Think of your mind as a vast ocean. Thoughts are the waves that constantly rise and fall. In mindfulness, we learn to become aware of those waves, recognizing their presence without being pulled under. It's like surfing – we ride the waves, experiencing their power, yet maintaining control.

Here's how mindfulness can help you manage stress and anxiety:

- **Increased Awareness:** Mindfulness sharpens your ability to recognize the early signs of stress or anxiety, like a tightening chest, racing heart, or furrowed brow. This early awareness allows you to intervene before these feelings escalate.

- **Reduced Overthinking:** The constant chatter of our thoughts can amplify stress and anxiety. Mindfulness encourages us to pause and observe these thoughts without judgment, allowing us to detach from their grip.

- **Improved Emotional Regulation:** By practicing mindfulness, we gain a better understanding of our emotions and their triggers. This awareness empowers us to regulate our emotions more effectively, preventing them from overwhelming us.

Simple Mindfulness Exercises:

- **Mindful Breathing:** Focus on your breath, inhaling and exhaling deeply. Notice the sensation of each breath entering and leaving your body.

- **Body Scan Meditation:** Pay attention to different parts of your body, starting from your toes and moving upward. Notice any sensations, such as tingling, warmth, or tension.

- **Mindful Walking:** Focus on the sensations of your feet touching the ground, the movement of your body, and the sights and sounds around you.

Relaxation Techniques for Stress Relief

Stress and anxiety often manifest physically, creating tension in our muscles, tightening our chest, and accelerating our heart rate. Relaxation techniques address these physical manifestations, promoting a sense of calm and well-being.

Deep Breathing Exercises:

Deep breathing exercises are a powerful tool for calming the nervous system. They involve inhaling deeply into your diaphragm, filling your lungs to capacity, and exhaling slowly and completely. This rhythmic breathing pattern sends a signal to your body that it's safe to relax.

Here's a simple deep breathing exercise:

1. **Sit comfortably:** Find a quiet place where you can sit upright with your back straight but relaxed.

2. **Close your eyes:** Gently close your eyes, focusing your attention inward.

3. **Inhale deeply:** Inhale slowly through your nose, allowing your abdomen to expand as your lungs fill with air.

4. **Hold for a few seconds:** Pause for a moment, holding your breath for a brief count.

5. **Exhale slowly:** Exhale slowly through your mouth, letting your abdomen contract as you release the air.

6. **Repeat:** Continue this deep breathing pattern for several minutes, noticing the calming effect it has on your body and mind.

Progressive Muscle Relaxation (PMR):

PMR is a technique that involves systematically tensing and releasing muscle groups throughout your body. By focusing on the physical sensations of tension and relaxation, you become more aware of your body's response to stress.

Here's a step-by-step guide to PMR:

1. **Find a comfortable position:** Lie down or sit in a comfortable chair with your arms and legs relaxed.

2. **Focus on your right hand:** Tighten the muscles in your right hand into a fist, holding the tension for a few seconds.

3. **Release the tension:** Gently release the tension in your hand, noticing the feeling of relaxation as the muscles soften.

4. **Repeat for other muscle groups:** Proceed to tense and release the muscles in your forearm, biceps, shoulders, forehead, jaw, neck, chest, abdomen, back, buttocks, thighs, calves, and feet.

5. **Scan your body:** After completing the sequence, take a moment to scan your entire body, noticing the overall feeling of relaxation.

Stress-Reduction Strategies for Everyday Life

Beyond specific techniques, incorporating stress-reduction strategies into your daily life can create a foundation for lasting emotional well-being.

Prioritize Sleep:

Adequate sleep is crucial for stress management. When you're sleep-deprived, your body releases cortisol, a stress hormone. Aim for 7-8 hours of quality sleep each night to help your body recover and rejuvenate.

Regular Exercise:

Physical activity is a natural stress reliever. Exercise releases endorphins, which have mood-boosting effects. Find an activity you enjoy, whether it's running, swimming, dancing, or yoga, and make it a regular part of your routine.

Healthy Diet:

What you eat affects how you feel. A balanced diet rich in fruits, vegetables, and whole grains provides your body with the nutrients it needs to function optimally. Avoid processed foods, excessive sugar, and caffeine, which can contribute to anxiety and stress.

Connect with Nature:

Spending time in nature has been shown to reduce stress and improve mood. Take a walk in the park, sit by a lake, or simply enjoy the beauty of your surroundings.

Practice Gratitude:

Focusing on the positive aspects of your life can shift your mindset and reduce stress. Take time each day to reflect on things you're grateful for, no matter how small they may seem.

Build a Support System:

Having strong relationships with family, friends, or a therapist can provide a safety net during stressful times. Share your feelings with loved ones, seek support from a therapist, or join a support group.

Set Boundaries:

Learning to say no when necessary is essential for managing stress. If you're feeling overwhelmed, don't hesitate to decline requests that will add to your workload or strain your resources.

Embrace the Present Moment:

Instead of dwelling on the past or worrying about the future, focus on the present moment. Be fully engaged in your current activity, whether it's work, a conversation, or simply enjoying a meal.

Learn to Forgive:

Holding onto grudges and resentment can create emotional turmoil and hinder your ability to move forward. Forgiveness is not about condoning harmful behavior but about releasing yourself from the burden of negativity.

Seek Professional Help:

If you're struggling to manage stress and anxiety on your own, don't hesitate to seek professional help. A therapist can provide guidance, support, and tools to help you navigate these challenges.

Remember, mastering your emotions is a lifelong journey. There will be moments of stress and anxiety, but the key is to develop the skills and strategies to manage them effectively. By practicing mindfulness, relaxation techniques, and incorporating stress-reduction strategies into your daily life, you can create a foundation for lasting emotional well-being. Embrace this journey of self-discovery, knowing that you have the power to cultivate a life filled with peace, joy, and resilience.

Cultivating Emotional Resilience

Imagine yourself standing on the edge of a storm, the wind whipping around you, the rain lashing against your face. The world feels tumultuous, unpredictable, and you might be tempted to retreat, to seek shelter from the chaos. But what if I told you that this storm, this turbulence, is actually an opportunity? An opportunity to discover a strength within you that you never knew existed, a resilience that will carry you through any challenge life throws your way.

This is the essence of emotional resilience: the ability to weather life's storms, to bounce back from setbacks, and to emerge stronger and more determined than before. It's not about being impervious to pain or hardship, but about learning to navigate those rough waters with grace and determination. It's about developing a deep well of inner strength that allows you to face adversity with courage and composure.

Think of emotional resilience as a muscle. Just like any muscle, it needs to be exercised and strengthened through consistent practice and effort. It's not something that happens overnight; it's a journey of self-discovery, a commitment to personal growth, and a conscious choice to embrace the challenges that life presents.

So, how do we cultivate this powerful resilience? How do we build that inner fortress that will protect us from the storms of life? Let's explore some powerful strategies that will empower you to navigate the emotional rollercoaster of life with grace and confidence.

1. Embrace the Power of Self-Awareness:

The first step towards building emotional resilience is to understand your own emotional landscape. It's about getting to know your triggers, your patterns of thinking, and how you typically react to stress and adversity. This isn't about judging yourself; it's about developing a deeper understanding of your emotional responses and how they impact your behavior.

Think of it as learning to read the language of your own emotions. Are you prone to anger, anxiety, or sadness? How do these emotions manifest in your thoughts, your words, and your actions? Once you become aware of your typical emotional patterns, you can start to identify the triggers that set them off and learn to manage them more effectively.

A simple but powerful tool for self-awareness is journaling. Take some time each day to reflect on your emotions. Write down what you're feeling, what triggered those feelings, and how those emotions impacted your behavior. Over time, you'll start to notice recurring patterns and gain a clearer understanding of your own emotional landscape.

2. Cultivate a Growth Mindset:

One of the most important ingredients for building emotional resilience is a growth mindset. This means believing that your abilities are not fixed but rather something that can be developed through effort and practice. When you embrace a growth mindset, you view setbacks not as failures but as opportunities to learn and grow.

Imagine a young child learning to walk. They stumble and fall, but they don't give up. Instead, they get back up, try again, and eventually learn to walk. This is the essence of a growth mindset. It's about embracing the process of learning, even when it's challenging or uncomfortable.

When you encounter a setback, instead of dwelling on the negative, ask yourself: "What can I learn from this experience? How can I use this as an opportunity to grow and improve?" This shift in perspective can transform your relationship with challenges and empower you to bounce back stronger than ever before.

3. Practice Mindfulness:

Mindfulness is the practice of paying attention to the present moment without judgment. It's about becoming aware of your thoughts, feelings, and sensations without getting caught up in them. Mindfulness can be a powerful tool for developing emotional resilience because it helps you to detach from your emotions and observe them with a sense of calm and clarity.

When you're caught up in a stressful situation, mindfulness can help you to step back and observe your emotions without getting swept away by them. This allows you to respond to the situation with greater awareness and composure, rather than reacting impulsively or allowing your emotions to control your behavior.

There are many different ways to practice mindfulness. Some people find it helpful to meditate, while others prefer to engage in mindful activities such as yoga, walking in nature, or simply paying attention to their senses while they eat or drink. Experiment with different mindfulness practices to find what works best for you.

4. Learn to Manage Stress:

Stress is an inevitable part of life, but chronic stress can have a devastating impact on your emotional well-being. It can lead to anxiety, depression, burnout, and weaken your ability to cope with challenges. Therefore, learning to manage stress effectively is crucial for building emotional resilience.

There are many different stress-management techniques that can be helpful, including exercise, relaxation techniques, and spending time in nature. Find what works best for you and make it a regular part of your routine.

Exercise is a powerful stress reliever, as it releases endorphins that have mood-boosting effects. Try to incorporate at least 30 minutes of moderate-intensity exercise most days of the week.

Relaxation techniques such as deep breathing exercises, progressive muscle relaxation, or meditation can also be very effective in reducing stress. These techniques help to calm the mind and body, reducing feelings of tension and anxiety.

Spending time in nature is another wonderful way to reduce stress. Being in nature can help to lower blood pressure, reduce heart rate, and promote feelings of calm and serenity.

5. Cultivate Gratitude:

Gratitude is a powerful emotion that can have a profound impact on your emotional well-being. When you focus on the positive aspects of your life, you shift your perspective from one of scarcity to one of abundance. This can help to reduce stress, boost happiness, and strengthen your ability to cope with challenges.

Take some time each day to reflect on the things you're grateful for. You can write them down in a journal, share them with loved ones, or simply take a few moments to appreciate them in your own mind. No matter how small or insignificant they may seem, make an effort to acknowledge the good things in your life.

6. Build Strong Relationships:

Strong relationships are a vital source of support and resilience. When you have a network of loving and supportive people in your life, you're more likely to feel connected, valued, and equipped to weather the storms of life.

Nurture your relationships with family, friends, and loved ones. Make time for them, listen to them, and let them know that you care. And don't be afraid to ask for help when you need it. Strong relationships can provide a powerful buffer against stress and adversity.

7. Forgive Yourself and Others:

Holding on to resentment and anger can be incredibly toxic. It can eat away at your emotional well-being and make it more difficult to cope with challenges. Forgiving yourself and others is an act of self-compassion and emotional liberation. It's about letting go of the past and creating space for healing, growth, and peace.

This doesn't mean condoning hurtful behavior or forgetting what happened. It means choosing to release the anger and resentment that you're holding onto. It's a conscious decision to move forward and create a brighter future for yourself.

8. Find Your Purpose:

Having a sense of purpose in life can provide a powerful anchor during difficult times. When you know why you're here and what you're striving for, you're more likely to stay focused and motivated, even when things get tough.

What are your passions? What brings you joy and fulfillment? What kind of impact do you want to make on the world? Once you identify your purpose, you can start to align your actions with your values and create a life that is truly meaningful.

9. Embrace the Power of Self-Care:

Self-care isn't about pampering or indulging; it's about taking care of your physical, mental, and emotional needs. It's about prioritizing your well-being and making sure that you're getting the rest, nourishment, and support that you need to thrive.

This might include things like getting enough sleep, eating healthy foods, exercising regularly, spending time in nature, pursuing hobbies, or spending time with loved ones. Make sure that you're carving out time for self-care in your daily routine.

10. Don't Be Afraid to Ask for Help:

One of the biggest mistakes people make when they're struggling is trying to go it alone. There's no shame in asking for help when you need it. Whether it's a friend, a family member, a therapist, or a support group, seeking out support can make a world of difference in your journey of building emotional resilience.

Remember that emotional resilience is a journey, not a destination. It's a lifelong process of learning, growing, and adapting. There will be ups and downs along the way, but by embracing the strategies outlined above, you can build a foundation of inner strength that will carry you through any challenge.

The Art of Letting Go

Imagine a heavy backpack, laden with burdens from the past. Each painful memory, each hurtful experience, each unresolved conflict, becomes a weight on your shoulders, pulling you down and preventing you from moving forward with ease. This backpack is the accumulation of negativity, a collection of hurts and resentments that we hold onto, often unknowingly, like a precious treasure. But what if we told you that this treasure is actually a burden, holding you back from experiencing the lightness and joy of a truly free spirit?

Forgiveness is the key to unlocking that backpack, releasing the heavy weight of past pain and opening the door to a world of possibilities. It is not about condoning the actions of others or forgetting the hurt they caused. Instead, it is about choosing to let go of the anger, bitterness, and resentment that we cling to. It is a conscious decision to break free from the chains of the past and step into the radiant light of the present moment.

Think of forgiveness as a gift you give yourself. By letting go of the negativity, you free yourself from its grip and create space for peace, joy, and love to flourish within you. The journey of forgiveness is not always easy. It takes courage, compassion, and a willingness to let go. It involves acknowledging the hurt, recognizing its impact on your life, and choosing to release it. It is a process of letting go, not just of the pain itself, but also of the person who caused it.

Here's a story that illustrates the power of forgiveness. Imagine a young girl, Emily, who was deeply hurt by a betrayal from her best friend, Sarah. The hurt ran deep, leaving Emily feeling betrayed and heartbroken. She carried the pain with her for months, constantly replaying the events in her mind, allowing the anger and resentment to consume her. She avoided Sarah, unable to forgive her and move on.

However, one day, Emily stumbled upon a quote that resonated with her: "Holding onto anger is like grasping a hot coal with the intent of throwing it at someone else; you are the one who gets burned." This quote sparked a shift in Emily's perspective. She realized that her anger was not only harming Sarah but also herself. It was a heavy burden she was carrying, weighing her down and preventing her from fully experiencing life.

Emily decided to take a leap of faith and practice forgiveness. It wasn't easy, but she started small. She began by acknowledging her own emotions, recognizing the pain and the anger. Then, she started to consider Sarah's perspective, trying to understand why she had acted the way she did. As she reflected more deeply, she realized that Sarah was going through her own struggles and that her actions were more a reflection of her own pain than a deliberate attempt to hurt Emily.

This realization opened the door to forgiveness. Emily understood that Sarah's betrayal was not solely about her. It was about Sarah's own journey and her own challenges. As Emily began to see Sarah's perspective, the anger and resentment slowly started to dissipate. The pain remained, but it no longer held the same power over her. She was finally able to release the burden, allowing the weight to fall away.

Emily's journey of forgiveness was not a sudden transformation but a gradual process of letting go. It took time, courage, and a willingness to shift her perspective. But the reward was immeasurable. By forgiving Sarah, Emily freed herself from the chains of negativity. She found peace, joy, and a sense of lightness she had not felt in a long time. She realized that forgiveness is not about forgetting the hurt; it is about choosing to release it, allowing yourself to move forward with a lighter heart and a brighter spirit.

Forgiveness is often misunderstood as a sign of weakness, but in reality, it is an act of immense strength. It takes immense courage to face the pain, acknowledge the hurt, and choose to release it. It is a testament to your resilience and your capacity to move forward, unburdened by the past.

Here are some practical steps you can take to practice the art of letting go:

1. **Acknowledge the hurt:** The first step towards forgiveness is acknowledging the pain. Don't suppress or deny your emotions.

Allow yourself to feel the hurt, the anger, and the resentment. Acknowledge the impact it has had on your life.

2. **Recognize your perspective:** Once you have acknowledged the hurt, take a step back and examine your own perspective. What are the thoughts and beliefs that are fueling your anger and resentment? Are you holding onto past grievances, refusing to move on?

3. **Consider the other person's perspective:** This may be a challenging step, especially if you are still feeling hurt or angry. But try to see things from the other person's perspective. What might have motivated their actions? What challenges might they be facing?

4. **Practice compassion:** Forgiveness is not about condoning the other person's actions but about choosing to let go of the anger and resentment that is holding you back. Practice compassion, recognizing that everyone makes mistakes and that everyone is struggling in their own way.

5. **Let go of the need for control:** Often, we hold onto anger and resentment because we want to control the situation or the person who hurt us. Let go of the need for control. Accept that you cannot change the past, and that you do not have the power to control other people.

6. **Focus on the present moment:** The past is gone, and the future is uncertain. The only moment you have control over is the present. By focusing on the present, you can let go of the past and start to create a more positive future.

7. **Engage in self-care:** Forgiveness can be a demanding process. Take care of yourself during this time. Engage in activities that bring you

joy, peace, and relaxation. Spend time with loved ones, practice mindfulness, and prioritize your well-being.

8. **Repeat as needed:** Forgiveness is not a one-time event. It is an ongoing process that requires patience, compassion, and a willingness to release the pain. If you find yourself slipping back into old patterns of anger and resentment, gently redirect your focus back to forgiveness.

Releasing negativity is a journey of self-discovery and empowerment. It is about reclaiming your power, releasing the burdens of the past, and creating space for peace, joy, and love to flourish within you. As you embark on this journey, remember that forgiveness is not a sign of weakness; it is an act of strength, compassion, and self-love. It is a gift you give yourself, freeing you from the chains of the past and allowing you to embrace a brighter, more fulfilling future.

Finding Joy and Purpose

Imagine a world where your emotions are your compass, guiding you toward a life filled with purpose and joy. It's a world where you understand your emotional landscape, manage stress and anxiety with ease, and cultivate resilience that helps you bounce back from setbacks. It's a world where you let go of past hurts, embrace forgiveness, and find the strength to create space for joy and peace. This, my friend, is the journey of mastering your emotions, and it's a journey that leads directly to the heart of finding your purpose in life.

We've explored the importance of emotional intelligence and self-awareness, recognizing the impact our emotions have on our thoughts and behaviors. We've learned about stress management techniques, mindfulness practices, and the art of cultivating resilience. We've even examined the power of forgiveness and letting go of past negativity. Now, it's time to uncover the profound connection between emotional well-being and finding purpose in life.

Think about it: when you're feeling overwhelmed by stress or consumed by anxiety, it's difficult to see beyond your immediate worries. Your mind is clouded, and it's hard to connect with your inner voice, the voice that whispers your deepest values and desires. But when you master your emotions, when you cultivate inner peace and a sense of calm, you open a door to self-discovery.

Imagine a serene lake reflecting the clear blue sky. When the waters are calm, you can see your reflection clearly, recognizing your own beauty and potential. But when the lake is agitated, the reflection is distorted, making it difficult to discern your true self. Your emotions are like the waters of the lake. When they are calm and balanced, you gain clarity and insight into your values, passions, and purpose. When they are turbulent, it's harder to see your path and find your direction.

Mastering your emotions is not about suppressing or ignoring them. It's about understanding them, accepting them, and learning to manage them effectively. When you're able to navigate the ups and downs of life with grace and resilience, you create a foundation for finding true joy and fulfilling your potential.

Connecting with Your Values

Finding purpose begins with understanding your values.

These are the core beliefs that guide your actions and decisions. They are the things that matter most to you, the principles that define your moral compass. Some common values include honesty, integrity, compassion, creativity, growth, family, community, and adventure. Take some time to reflect on your own life. What are the values that are most important to you?

Think about the moments in your life where you felt most alive, most fulfilled. What were you doing? What qualities did you embody? What values were in play? These are clues to your deepest desires, the things that truly matter to you. It's like a treasure map leading you to your purpose.

Once you've identified your core values, it's time to start living in alignment with them. This means making choices that reflect your beliefs and aspirations. It means saying "no" to things that don't align with your values, even if they seem appealing or convenient. It means prioritizing the things that matter most to you, even if it means sacrificing something else.

Living in alignment with your values doesn't mean being rigid or inflexible. It means creating a life that is true to your heart, a life that brings you joy and fulfillment. It means making choices that resonate with your soul.

Discovering Activities that Bring You Joy

The next step in finding purpose is to explore activities that bring you joy. These are the things that light you up, that make you feel energized and inspired. They are the activities that you could do for hours on end without feeling bored or drained.

Think about your hobbies, interests, and past experiences. What did you enjoy as a child? What activities still bring you a spark of excitement? Don't be afraid to step outside of your comfort zone and try something new. You might be surprised to discover hidden passions or talents you never knew you had.

It's important to be open and curious as you explore different activities. Pay attention to how you feel when you're engaged in a particular activity. Do you feel energized, focused, or inspired? Does it bring you a sense of peace, purpose, or creativity? The activities that evoke these positive emotions are likely to be aligned with your purpose.

Finding Meaning in Your Work

For many people, work is a significant part of their lives. Finding meaning in your work is a powerful way to connect with your purpose. It's not about finding a job that's easy or glamorous, but about finding work that aligns with your values and passions. Ask yourself these questions:

- What kind of impact do I want to make on the world?
- What kind of work makes me feel fulfilled and energized?
- How can I use my skills and talents to make a difference?

If your current work isn't fulfilling your purpose, it may be time to explore other options. Perhaps you can transition into a different role within your current company or consider a career change altogether. Remember, your purpose is not limited to your job. It can be found in all aspects of your life, including your hobbies, volunteer work, or even your relationships.

Creating a Life of Purpose

Finding purpose is a journey, not a destination. It's a constant process of self-discovery, exploration, and evolution. There will be times when you feel lost or uncertain, but those moments are opportunities for growth and reflection. Embrace the journey, and remember that your purpose is ever evolving.

Here are some practical steps you can take to create a life of purpose:

- **Set intentions:** Start each day with a clear intention of what you want to accomplish. This could be something as simple as "I will be present and grateful today" or "I will focus on my passions."

- **Practice mindfulness:** Take time each day to simply be present in the moment. Observe your thoughts and feelings without judgment. Mindfulness helps you connect with your inner voice and understand what truly matters to you.

- **Seek out mentors and role models:** Connect with people who have found their purpose in life. Ask them questions, seek their advice, and learn from their experiences.

- **Embrace challenges:** Challenges are opportunities for growth and learning. Don't shy away from them. Instead, see them as opportunities to develop your resilience, creativity, and resourcefulness.

- **Give back to your community:** Find ways to make a difference in the lives of others. Volunteering, mentoring, or donating to a cause that you care about can bring a profound sense of purpose and fulfillment.

The journey of finding purpose is a beautiful one. It's a journey of self-discovery, growth, and connection. By mastering your emotions, understanding your values, and exploring activities that bring you joy, you can create a life that is truly fulfilling and aligned with your deepest aspirations. Remember, you have the power to create a life of purpose, joy, and meaning. Embrace the journey, and let your heart guide you.

CHAPTER 4
THE POWER OF SELF-CARE

Prioritizing Your Wellbeing

Imagine a world where you prioritize your well-being as if it were a cherished treasure, a radiant jewel you'd safeguard with all your heart. This is the essence of self-care, a profound act of love and respect for the extraordinary being you are. Self-care isn't about indulgence – it's not a fleeting escape from reality. It's a fundamental pillar of a life brimming with energy, joy, and resilience. It's the fertile ground from which your dreams, aspirations, and deepest desires can flourish.

Think of self-care as a symphony of practices that nourish your physical, mental, and emotional well-being. It's about listening attentively to your body's whispers, understanding the nuances of your emotions, and creating a space where your mind can rest and recharge. It's about making conscious choices that honor your needs, values, and aspirations, day after day.

Why is self-care so crucial? Because when you neglect your well-being, you risk depleting your reserves of energy, vitality, and resilience. Imagine a car with an empty gas tank or a garden left to wither under the scorching sun. That's what happens to you when you consistently prioritize everything else but yourself. You lose the ability to show up fully in your life, to meet challenges with strength and grace, and to experience the fullness of your potential.

Think of a grand oak tree, rooted deep in the earth, its branches stretching towards the heavens. The tree's resilience lies in its ability to draw nourishment from the earth, to stand firm against the storms, and to continue growing year after year. You are the oak tree, and self-care is the nourishing earth that sustains you.

Imagine the life you could live when you prioritize your well-being:

- **Physical Health:** You wake up each morning with a renewed sense of energy, eager to embrace the day. Your body feels strong and agile, ready to move with ease and grace. You have a radiant glow that emanates from a healthy and well-nourished body. You cultivate healthy habits that become a natural part of your life, like regular exercise, mindful eating, and deep, restful sleep. Your body becomes a temple you cherish and honor.

- **Mental Clarity:** Your mind is a sanctuary of peace and tranquility. You have the ability to focus, concentrate, and access your creative potential with ease. Negative thoughts are no longer your constant companions. You've learned to identify and challenge them with positive affirmations and compassionate self-talk. Your mind is a space of clarity, strength, and empowerment.

- **Emotional Well-being:** You navigate the ups and downs of life with a newfound resilience. You can recognize and express your emotions healthily, embracing both joy and sorrow. You've cultivated a deep sense of self-acceptance and self-compassion, allowing you to meet challenges with courage and grace. You are no longer ruled by your emotions, but rather a mindful observer of your emotional landscape.

But self-care isn't about indulging in momentary pleasures. It's not about binge-watching TV, overeating, or constantly seeking external validation. True self-care is a conscious and deliberate act of love and respect for your well-being. It's about making sustainable choices that nourish your body, mind, and spirit.

Let's explore the difference between true self-care and self-indulgence:

Self-indulgence:

- **Focuses on fleeting pleasures:** Self-indulgence often centers around short-term gratifications that might feel good in the moment but don't contribute to lasting well-being. It might involve overeating, excessive shopping, or engaging in unhealthy habits.

- **Driven by guilt and shame:** Self-indulgence often arises from a desire to escape unpleasant feelings, leading to guilt and shame after the fleeting pleasure fades. It's a cycle of momentary escape followed by regret.

- **Leads to depletion:** Self-indulgence can lead to a depletion of energy, resources, and motivation, ultimately leaving you feeling worse than before. It's like a quick fix that provides temporary relief but fails to address the underlying issues.

True Self-care:

- **Prioritizes long-term well-being:** True self-care focuses on practices that nourish your physical, mental, and emotional health in a sustainable way. It's about making choices that support your long-term goals and aspirations.

- **Driven by self-love and respect:** True self-care is fueled by a deep love and respect for yourself. It's about recognizing your needs and making choices that honor those needs, even when it might feel challenging or uncomfortable.

- **Leads to growth and empowerment:** True self-care empowers you to take charge of your life and create a life that is fulfilling and meaningful. It's about investing in your well-being, knowing that it's the foundation for everything you do.

So, how do you begin your journey of self-care?

- **Listen to your body's whispers:** Pay attention to the signals your body is sending. Are you feeling fatigued, stressed, or out of balance? Notice the sensations, the emotions, and the subtle messages your body is trying to convey.

- **Identify your needs:** What are the things you need to feel your best? Do you need more rest, movement, connection, or time for creative pursuits? Be honest with yourself about what nourishes you and what depletes you.

- **Prioritize your well-being:** Treat self-care as a non-negotiable. Schedule time for activities that bring you joy, relaxation, and a sense of purpose.

- **Embrace small changes:** Don't try to do everything at once. Start with small, manageable changes and gradually build upon them.

- **Be patient and compassionate:** The journey of self-care is a marathon, not a sprint. Be patient with yourself, celebrate your progress, and remember that you are worth the effort.

Think of self-care as an ongoing conversation with yourself. It's a dialogue of listening, understanding, and responding to your needs in a loving and compassionate way. It's about creating a life that feels aligned with your values and aspirations, a life where you can flourish and thrive.

Remember, you are a magnificent creation, deserving of love, care, and attention. Embrace the journey of self-care and discover the extraordinary potential that lies within you.

Creating a Self Care Routine

Imagine a world where you wake up feeling refreshed and energized, ready to embrace the day with a sense of purpose and calm. A world where you prioritize your needs, nourishing your body, mind, and soul. This is the world of self-care, a world that's not about indulgence but about intentional actions that empower you to thrive.

Self-care is about recognizing that you are worthy of love, attention, and care. It's about understanding that you can't pour from an empty cup, and that taking care of yourself isn't selfish, but rather a necessary act of self-preservation. In a world that constantly demands our attention, it's easy to neglect our own well-being. Self-care is a powerful antidote to this relentless pace, offering a pathway to a life of greater balance, joy, and fulfillment.

So, how do you create a self-care routine that truly serves you? It's a personal journey, unique to each individual. There's no one-size-fits-all approach, but a few guiding principles can help you create a routine that nourishes your body, mind, and soul.

1. Listen to Your Body's Whispers:

Start by tuning in to your body's signals. What does it crave? What does it need to feel balanced and vibrant? Perhaps it's a good night's sleep, a nourishing meal, or simply some time spent in nature. Maybe you're craving physical activity, creative expression, or a moment of quiet contemplation. Pay attention to the subtle whispers of your body, and honor its requests.

2. Embrace the Power of Routine:

Routines provide a sense of structure and consistency, making it easier to prioritize self-care. Think of it as a framework, a gentle reminder to check in with yourself and meet your needs. Your routine can be as simple or as complex as you like, but it should be something you can realistically maintain.

3. Create a Menu of Self-Care Practices:

Think of self-care as a buffet, a diverse selection of practices that address your physical, mental, and emotional well-being. Here's a starting point:

Physical Self-Care:

- **Movement:** Find ways to move your body that you enjoy. Whether it's yoga, dancing, swimming, or simply taking a walk in nature, movement can boost your energy, reduce stress, and improve your overall mood.

- **Nutrition:** Nourish your body with healthy, wholesome foods. Pay attention to how different foods make you feel, and choose options that energize you rather than drain you.

- **Sleep:** Prioritize sleep! A good night's rest is essential for physical and mental rejuvenation. Aim for 7-9 hours of quality sleep each night.

- **Hygiene:** Simple practices like showering, brushing your teeth, and getting dressed can have a positive impact on your mood and self-esteem.

Mental Self-Care:

- **Mindfulness:** Cultivate mindfulness through practices like meditation, deep breathing, or simply paying attention to the present moment without judgment. Mindfulness can help you manage stress, anxiety, and negative thoughts.
- **Creative Expression:** Engage in activities that allow you to tap into your creative side. Whether it's painting, writing, playing music, or simply spending time in nature, creativity can be a powerful way to reduce stress and boost your mood.
- **Reading:** Reading can be a relaxing and enriching activity. Choose books that inspire you, transport you, or provide new insights.
- **Learning:** Learning new things can stimulate your mind and keep you feeling engaged. Take a class, listen to a podcast, or read a book on a topic that interests you.

Emotional Self-Care:

- **Journaling:** Journaling is a powerful tool for processing emotions, gaining self-awareness, and identifying patterns in your thoughts and behaviors.
- **Connection:** Spend time with loved ones and cultivate meaningful relationships. Human connection is essential for emotional well-being.
- **Nature:** Spending time in nature has been shown to have a profound impact on mental and emotional well-being. Take a walk in the park, go for a hike, or simply sit under a tree and enjoy the fresh air and sunshine.

- **Setting Boundaries:** Learn to set healthy boundaries to protect your emotional well-being. This means saying no to things that drain you and prioritizing activities that nourish you.

4. Experiment and Adapt:

Self-care is an ongoing process of discovery. As you experiment with different practices, you'll learn what works best for you. Be flexible and adaptable, and don't be afraid to change things up if something isn't serving you.

5. Be Kind to Yourself:

Self-care is not about perfection. It's about showing up for yourself, even when you don't feel like it. Be gentle with yourself and practice self-compassion. You are worthy of care and love, just as you are.

6. Schedule It In:

Once you've identified your self-care practices, schedule them into your day. Just like you would schedule important appointments, schedule time for self-care. This will help you prioritize it and make it a regular part of your routine.

7. Celebrate Your Wins:

Celebrate your small wins along the way. Acknowledge the progress you're making and recognize how much you're caring for yourself. This will help you stay motivated and committed to your self-care journey.

Examples of Self-Care Routines:

Routine 1: The Mindful Morning:

- **Wake up early:** Give yourself ample time to start your day calmly.
- **Mindful Meditation:** Practice 10-15 minutes of meditation to center your mind and set a positive intention for the day.

- **Hydration:** Drink a glass of water to rehydrate after sleep.
- **Healthy Breakfast:** Enjoy a nourishing breakfast that provides energy and nutrients.
- **Movement:** Go for a walk, do some stretches, or engage in a light workout.

Routine 2: The Evening Relaxation:

- **Unwind:** Dim the lights, put on some soothing music, and create a relaxing atmosphere.
- **Warm Bath:** Soak in a warm bath with essential oils or Epsom salts.
- **Journaling:** Write down your thoughts and feelings, releasing any tension or stress.
- **Reading:** Read a book or magazine that you enjoy.
- **Early Bedtime:** Aim for 7-9 hours of sleep.

Routine 3: The Weekend Retreat:

- **Sleep In:** Give yourself permission to sleep in and catch up on rest.
- **Nature Walk:** Spend time in nature, whether it's hiking, walking, or simply sitting under a tree.
- **Creative Activity:** Engage in an activity that allows you to express your creativity, such as painting, writing, or playing music.
- **Connection:** Spend time with loved ones, engaging in activities that you enjoy together.

- **Self-Care Ritual:** Create a special self-care ritual that you can do on the weekends, such as a face mask, a massage, or a meditation session.

Creating a Self-Care Routine:

Here's a step-by-step guide to create a personalized self-care routine:

1. Identify Your Needs:

Reflect on your current life and identify areas where you feel stressed, overwhelmed, or depleted.

Ask yourself: What do I need to feel my best? What brings me joy? What brings me peace?

2. Choose Your Practices:

Explore different self-care practices and choose those that resonate with you.

Consider your preferences, lifestyle, and resources.

3. Create a Schedule:

Allocate specific time slots for your chosen self-care practices.

Be realistic about how much time you can commit and set achievable goals.

4. Start Small:

Don't try to do too much at once.

Begin with one or two practices and gradually add more as you feel comfortable.

5. Be Flexible:

Allow yourself to adjust your routine as needed.

Be open to new practices and experiment to find what works best for you.

6. Be Patient:

It takes time to develop a consistent self-care routine.

Be patient with yourself and celebrate your progress along the way.

Remember, self-care is an act of love and kindness towards yourself. It's about prioritizing your well-being and creating a life that is both fulfilling and sustainable. By creating a personalized self-care routine, you are investing in your own happiness, health, and success.

The Importance of Rest and Relaxation

In the tapestry of life, rest and relaxation are not mere indulgences, but essential threads that weave together our well-being. Just as a plant needs sunlight, water, and fertile soil to flourish, our bodies and minds need periods of rest to recharge, rejuvenate, and thrive. In a world that often demands constant productivity and achievement, it's easy to neglect the importance of rest. However, embracing the power of rest is not a sign of weakness, but a testament to our commitment to holistic well-being.

Imagine yourself as a marathon runner. You train rigorously, push your limits, and strive for victory. But what happens when you forget to fuel your body, hydrate, and give it time to recover? You risk exhaustion, injury, and ultimately, failure. The same principle applies to our lives. If we constantly push ourselves without allowing for rest, we risk burnout, decreased productivity, and a decline in our overall quality of life.

The benefits of getting enough sleep are profound. Sleep is not merely a passive state; it's a vital biological process that repairs and restores our bodies and minds. During sleep, our brains consolidate memories, clear out toxins, and regulate hormones. Adequate sleep enhances cognitive function, improves mood, strengthens the immune system, and boosts our ability to cope with stress. Chronic sleep deprivation, on the other hand, can lead to a cascade of negative consequences, including impaired concentration, poor decision-making, increased risk of chronic diseases, and even accidents.

The quality of our sleep is just as important as the quantity. Creating a conducive sleep environment is key. This involves establishing a regular sleep schedule, ensuring a dark, quiet, and cool bedroom, avoiding caffeine and alcohol before bedtime, and engaging in relaxing activities before sleep, such as reading or taking a warm bath. It's also important to be mindful of our digital detox, as the blue light emitted from electronic devices can interfere with melatonin production, a hormone that regulates sleep cycles.

Beyond sleep, practicing relaxation techniques is crucial for our well-being. Our modern lives are filled with constant stimuli, demands, and pressures that can lead to chronic stress and anxiety. Relaxation techniques like deep breathing exercises, meditation, yoga, or progressive muscle relaxation help to calm the nervous system, lower heart rate, and reduce stress hormones. These techniques provide a much-needed break from the relentless cycle of "fight-or-flight" responses, allowing us to enter a state of deep relaxation and restore our mental and emotional balance.

Think of relaxation as a mental vacation. Just as we need physical vacations to escape our daily routines and recharge our batteries, our minds need mental breaks to de-stress and reconnect with our inner selves. When we practice relaxation techniques, we create space for clarity, creativity, and a renewed sense of perspective. It's like hitting the "refresh" button on our minds, allowing us to approach life's challenges with renewed energy, focus, and resilience.

Beyond sleep and relaxation techniques, taking time for rest and rejuvenation is essential. This involves creating opportunities for leisure activities, hobbies, and pursuits that bring us joy and fulfillment. Whether it's spending time in nature, listening to music, pursuing a creative passion, or simply reading a good book, these activities provide a much-needed escape from the demands of everyday life. They nourish our souls, spark our creativity, and allow us to reconnect with our true selves.

Remember, rest and rejuvenation are not selfish acts, but essential investments in our overall well-being. They are the foundation upon which we build a life of meaning, purpose, and joy. By prioritizing rest, we are not just taking care of ourselves, but also nurturing our capacity to contribute to the world in a positive and meaningful way. So, embrace the power of rest. Give yourself permission to recharge, rejuvenate, and experience the transformative benefits of a well-rested body and mind.

Nurturing Your Physical Health

Do you know that feeling of being sluggish, tired, and just not quite yourself? It's a signal your body is trying to send you a message that whispers, "Hey, it's time to pay attention to me!" Taking care of your physical health isn't just about looking good in a swimsuit; it's about feeling good from the inside out, about having the energy to pursue your passions, and about being present and engaged in life's adventures.

Think of your body as a magnificent machine, a complex and intricate network of systems designed to carry you through every moment of your journey. Like any machine, it needs regular maintenance to run smoothly. This means fueling it with the right kind of nourishment, giving it a chance to rest and recharge, and keeping it active and strong.

Imagine a car you've neglected, filled with junk food instead of clean fuel, left parked in the garage for weeks, and never taken for a good spin. It's likely to sputter, wheeze, and eventually break down. Your body is no different. If you constantly neglect it, it will send you warning signs. You might experience fatigue, sluggishness, aches and pains, mood swings, and difficulty concentrating. These are your body's cries for help, its way of saying, "Hey, I need some love!"

Fueling Your Body for Success

Just like a car needs high-quality fuel to run efficiently, your body needs the right kind of nourishment to function at its best. It's not about restrictive diets or depriving yourself of the foods you enjoy; it's about making mindful choices that fuel your body with the energy it needs to thrive.

Think of your plate as a canvas for a masterpiece. Fill it with vibrant colors, fresh ingredients, and a variety of textures. Imagine a symphony of flavors that nourish your body and delight your senses. This could mean embracing vibrant fruits and vegetables, lean protein sources, whole grains, and healthy fats.

Imagine yourself reaching for a crisp apple instead of a sugary pastry. Feel the satisfaction of a hearty bowl of lentil soup instead of a greasy burger. Picture yourself sipping a refreshing green smoothie instead of a sugary soda. These small, intentional choices can make a big difference in how you feel.

Exercise: Your Body's Elixir

Now, picture this: You're feeling stressed, anxious, or just plain blah. You're stuck in a mental rut, and your creativity feels stagnant. What can you do to break free? The answer might surprise you: it's as simple as moving your body!

Exercise isn't just about building muscle; it's about boosting your mood, enhancing your cognitive function, and creating a sense of well-being. It's like a magical elixir that helps your body and mind work in harmony.

Think of exercise as a form of meditation, a way to connect with your body and clear your mind. It can be as simple as a brisk walk in nature, a dance session in your living room, or a yoga practice that helps you stretch and find inner peace.

The key is to find an activity you enjoy and incorporate it into your routine. Maybe you find solace in the rhythm of running, the calming flow of swimming, or the strength-building power of weightlifting. Whatever sparks your interest, embrace it!

The Power of Rest and Rejuvenation

Think of your body like a flower. Just as a flower needs sunlight, water, and nourishment to bloom, your body needs rest and rejuvenation to thrive. This doesn't just mean getting enough sleep; it's about giving yourself permission to relax, unwind, and recharge.

Imagine yourself curling up with a good book, taking a long, hot bath, or enjoying a peaceful walk in nature. These simple acts of self-care can work wonders for your body and mind. They allow your body to rest, repair, and rejuvenate, giving you the energy to face the day with renewed vigor.

Creating a Holistic Approach to Health

Taking care of your physical health is not about following rigid rules or striving for unrealistic ideals. It's about cultivating a holistic approach that encompasses all aspects of your well-being. It's about listening to your body's cues and responding with love, compassion, and respect.

Think of it as a journey of self-discovery, a process of understanding your unique needs and creating a lifestyle that supports your overall health and happiness.

Listen to Your Body's Whispers

Your body is a powerful vessel that carries you through life's adventures. It's a source of strength, resilience, and joy. Listen to its whispers, pay attention to its signals, and respond with love and care.

Embrace the transformative power of movement, nourishment, rest, and rejuvenation. Discover the joy of feeling healthy, energized, and alive.

Remember, taking care of your physical health is an act of self-love, an investment in your well-being, and a commitment to living a life filled with purpose and passion.

Connecting with Nature and the Outdoors

Imagine yourself standing on the edge of a sun-drenched meadow, the scent of wildflowers filling your nostrils. You feel the soft caress of a gentle breeze against your skin, the warmth of the sun on your face. As you take a deep breath, you're enveloped by the serenity of nature, a feeling of peace and tranquility washing over you. This, my friend, is the power of connecting with nature and the outdoors.

It's a powerful reminder that there's a world beyond our screens, our concrete jungles, and our daily routines. It's a world that speaks to the primal parts of us, the parts that yearn for connection, for a sense of belonging, and for a moment of pure, unadulterated joy.

The benefits of spending time in nature are undeniable. It's a natural stress reliever, a mood booster, and a source of inspiration. It can quiet the incessant chatter of our minds, allowing us to reconnect with ourselves, to find clarity, and to tap into our creativity.

Think about it: when was the last time you truly felt at peace? When was the last time you felt truly connected to something larger than yourself? For many of us, the answer lies in the embrace of nature.

A Breath of Fresh Air

The act of simply breathing fresh air can work wonders for our mental and emotional well-being. The air in nature is cleaner, less polluted, and richer in oxygen. With every inhale, we're filling our bodies with life-giving energy, revitalizing our minds and invigorating our spirits.

Think of it as a natural detox, a way to cleanse ourselves of the stresses and toxins that build up in our daily lives. The feeling of fresh air against our lungs is a reminder that we're alive, that we're connected to the world around us, and that we're part of something larger than ourselves.

Connecting with Our Inner Selves

Spending time in nature allows us to escape the hustle and bustle of modern life, to step away from the constant barrage of stimuli and distractions. It gives us the space and quiet we need to connect with our inner selves, to listen to our intuition, and to find clarity in our thoughts.

Think about it: when you're surrounded by the grandeur of a mountain range, the vastness of an ocean, or the delicate beauty of a forest, you're less likely to be consumed by your own worries. Nature has a way of reminding us of our place in the grand scheme of things, putting our problems into perspective and helping us to find a sense of peace.

Rejuvenating Our Minds and Bodies

The beauty of nature has a restorative effect on our minds and bodies. It helps to reduce stress hormones, lower blood pressure, and improve our overall sense of well-being. Studies have shown that spending time in nature can even boost our immune system, making us less susceptible to illness.

Think of it as a natural antidepressant, a way to lift our spirits and improve our overall health. Nature provides a sense of wonder and awe that can rejuvenate our minds and bodies, making us feel more energized, more alive, and more connected to the world around us.

The Power of Nature's Rhythms

Nature operates on its own rhythms, a cycle of day and night, seasons, and growth. When we immerse ourselves in nature, we become attuned to these natural rhythms, allowing us to find a sense of balance and harmony in our own lives.

Think about it: the changing seasons provide a natural framework for our lives, reminding us to slow down during the colder months and to embrace the energy and growth of spring and summer. The rising and setting of the sun provides a natural rhythm for our sleep-wake cycle, helping us to find a sense of balance between activity and rest.

Finding Inspiration in Nature's Art

Nature is an artist, a master of creativity and beauty. From the delicate petals of a wildflower to the towering majesty of a mountain range, nature is filled with inspiration for all who seek it.

Think about it: the intricate patterns of a snowflake, the vibrant colors of a sunset, the graceful movement of a bird in flight – all these things can spark our creativity, providing us with new ideas, new perspectives, and a renewed sense of wonder.

Expanding Our World View

Spending time in nature can help us to broaden our perspective, to see the world from a different point of view. It can challenge our assumptions, open our minds to new possibilities, and help us to appreciate the interconnectedness of all living things.

Think about it: when we're surrounded by the vastness of nature, we're less likely to be consumed by our own small concerns. We begin to see the world as a tapestry of life, a complex and interconnected system where every creature plays a vital role.

Creating a Deeper Connection

Connecting with nature isn't just about getting some fresh air or enjoying a scenic view. It's about developing a deeper connection to the world around us, a sense of belonging and responsibility.

Think about it: when we appreciate the beauty and wonder of nature, we're more likely to want to protect it, to care for it, and to leave it better than we found it. This sense of connection and responsibility can inspire us to make positive changes in our own lives, to live in harmony with nature, and to contribute to a healthier and more sustainable future.

Nature as a Sanctuary

For many of us, nature provides a sanctuary, a place to escape the stresses of daily life and find a sense of peace and tranquility. It's a place where we can be ourselves, where we can let go of our worries, and where we can reconnect with our true selves.

Think about it: the sound of waves crashing on the shore, the rustling of leaves in the wind, the gentle murmur of a stream – all these sounds can have a calming effect on our minds and bodies, helping us to relax and unwind. Nature provides a sense of serenity and peace that we can't find anywhere else.

Practical Ways to Connect with Nature

You don't need to go on a wilderness expedition to experience the benefits of nature. There are many simple ways to connect with the natural world, even if you live in a busy city.

- **Take a walk in the park:** Even a short walk in a local park can help to reduce stress, improve your mood, and connect you with nature.

- **Go for a hike:** Hiking is a great way to get exercise, enjoy fresh air, and experience the beauty of the outdoors.

- **Spend time in your garden:** Gardening is a great way to connect with nature, get some exercise, and grow your own food.

- **Sit outside and enjoy the view:** Even just sitting outside and enjoying the fresh air and the sights and sounds of nature can have a positive impact on your well-being.

- **Observe nature:** Take time to observe the natural world around you, from the intricate details of a flower to the flight of a bird.

The Gift of Nature

Connecting with nature is a gift, a gift that can enrich our lives in countless ways. It's a gift that can help us to reduce stress, improve our mood, boost our creativity, and find a deeper sense of peace and fulfillment.

So, the next time you're feeling stressed, overwhelmed, or disconnected, take a moment to step outside and connect with the natural world. You'll be surprised at how much better you feel.

Remember, nature is a powerful source of healing, inspiration, and joy. Embrace its power, and let it guide you on your journey of self-discovery and personal growth.

CHAPTER 5

BUILDING STRONG RELATIONSHIPS

The Importance of Healthy Relationships

Imagine a garden, bursting with vibrant flowers, each unique in its hue and fragrance. Some thrive in the sun, others in the shade, but they all depend on each other for growth and sustenance. These flowers represent the relationships we cultivate in our lives. Just as a garden flourishes with a diverse array of flowers, our lives become richer and more fulfilling when we nurture a variety of meaningful connections.

Relationships are not simply social amenities; they are the lifeblood of our well-being and personal growth. They provide us with a sense of belonging, support, and purpose. They act as mirrors, reflecting back to us our strengths, weaknesses, and blind spots. Through the lens of our relationships, we gain insights into ourselves that we might never have discovered alone.

Think of a time when you were feeling lost or unsure. Who did you turn to for comfort, guidance, or a listening ear? Perhaps it was a close friend, a family member, or a trusted mentor. These relationships provided a safe space for you to process your emotions, explore your thoughts, and gain new perspectives. They offered you a sense of connection and reminded you that you are not alone in your journey.

Nurturing meaningful connections goes beyond simply maintaining a social circle. It requires intentionality, vulnerability, and a genuine desire to connect with others on a deeper level. It involves listening attentively, offering support, and being present in the moments that matter. It means celebrating each other's successes, offering solace during times of difficulty, and being there for each other through thick and thin.

Strong relationships are not built overnight. They require time, effort, and a commitment to nurturing mutual understanding, respect, and trust. Just like a garden needs tending, relationships need consistent attention, watering, and weeding out negative patterns or behaviors that may hinder their growth.

One of the most essential elements of healthy relationships is the ability to communicate openly and honestly. This involves expressing your thoughts and feelings, both positive and negative, in a respectful and constructive manner. It also means being a good listener, actively seeking to understand the other person's perspective, even if it differs from your own.

Setting boundaries is another crucial aspect of fostering healthy relationships. Boundaries are like fences that define the parameters of what is acceptable and unacceptable behavior. They protect our emotional and physical well-being and prevent us from feeling overwhelmed or taken advantage of. It's important to communicate our boundaries clearly and assertively, while also respecting the boundaries of others.

Empathy and compassion are the cornerstones of strong relationships. Empathy allows us to step into another person's shoes and see the world from their perspective. Compassion fuels our desire to offer support, comfort, and understanding to those who are hurting or struggling. When we cultivate empathy and compassion, we create a foundation of mutual respect and understanding that strengthens our bonds and deepens our connections.

Remember, relationships are a two-way street. We cannot expect to receive without giving. It's essential to invest in our relationships, showing appreciation, gratitude, and affection to those who matter most. Small gestures, like a thoughtful card, a heartfelt phone call, or simply spending quality time together, can go a long way in strengthening our bonds and nurturing a sense of love and connection.

Relationships are a powerful force in our lives, capable of shaping our thoughts, feelings, and behaviors. They can either uplift us or weigh us down, depending on the quality of our connections. By nurturing healthy relationships, we create a support system that helps us navigate the challenges of life, celebrate our successes, and grow into the best versions of ourselves.

Just as a gardener tends to their plants with care, we must tend to our relationships with intentionality, compassion, and a willingness to learn and grow. By cultivating a garden of strong and meaningful relationships, we create a haven of love, support, and belonging that enriches our lives and helps us flourish.

Setting Boundaries and Saying No

Imagine a world where your needs and desires are respected, where you feel comfortable expressing your opinions, and where you are empowered to say "no" without fear of judgment or guilt. This is the world of healthy boundaries, a vital ingredient in building strong and fulfilling relationships.

Setting boundaries is not about being selfish or uncaring; it's about protecting your emotional and mental well-being. When you establish clear boundaries, you communicate to others what you are and are not willing to tolerate. It's like putting up a fence around your personal space, letting people know where the line is, and what they can and cannot cross.

Think of a boundary as a way of creating a safe and secure space for yourself. It's a way of saying, "This is who I am, and this is what I need to thrive." Just as a fence protects a garden, boundaries protect your emotional garden from being trampled upon.

But how do you actually set boundaries? It's not as daunting as it may seem. It begins with self-awareness and understanding your own needs and values. What are your non-negotiables? What are you comfortable with, and what are you not comfortable with? Once you have a clear understanding of your personal boundaries, you need to learn how to communicate them effectively.

The Art of Saying No

Saying "no" is an essential skill in setting boundaries. It's a way of asserting your right to choose what you want and don't want. Unfortunately, many people struggle with saying "no" because they fear disappointing others, causing conflict, or being perceived as selfish. But saying "no" is not about hurting others; it's about taking care of yourself.

Communicating Your Boundaries Assertively

Communicating your boundaries assertively is key to ensuring they are respected. Assertiveness means being able to express your needs and feelings clearly, respectfully, and confidently, without resorting to aggression or passivity. It's about finding a balance between being respectful of others' feelings while also advocating for your own.

Here are some tips for communicating your boundaries assertively:

- **Be direct and clear:** State your boundaries in a clear and concise manner. For example, instead of saying "I'm not really sure if I can do that," try saying "I'm not available to help with that right now."

- **Use "I" statements:** "I" statements help you take ownership of your feelings and needs, rather than blaming or accusing others. For example, instead of saying "You always interrupt me," try saying "I feel disrespected when I'm interrupted."

- **Be firm and consistent:** It's important to be firm and consistent in upholding your boundaries. If you waver or give in easily, others will continue to push your limits.

- **Set consequences:** When you set a boundary, it's important to communicate the consequences of crossing that line. This helps others understand the seriousness of your boundary and the potential impact of their actions.

- **Practice active listening:** When someone is trying to push your boundaries, it's important to actively listen to what they are saying. This can help you better understand their perspective and respond in a more thoughtful way.

Examples of Setting Boundaries in Relationships

Here are some real-life examples of how to set boundaries in different types of relationships:

- **Romantic Relationships:** If your partner is constantly demanding your attention or making you feel pressured to do things you don't want to do, it's important to set boundaries. This might involve saying "no" to certain activities, setting time aside for your own needs, or establishing clear expectations around communication and intimacy.

- **Family Relationships:** Family relationships can be challenging when it comes to boundaries. You might need to set boundaries around topics of conversation, financial support, or time spent together. For example, you might need to say "no" to requests that drain your energy or violate your values.

- **Friendships:** Friendships are also an area where healthy boundaries are essential. You might need to set boundaries around gossiping, lending money, or being there for someone who constantly needs rescuing.

- **Work Relationships:** In the workplace, it's important to set boundaries around your work schedule, your responsibilities, and your interactions with colleagues. This might involve saying "no" to additional tasks, setting clear expectations around deadlines, or establishing clear communication channels.

Dealing with Boundary Pushers

Setting boundaries can sometimes lead to conflict, especially with people who are used to pushing your limits. It's important to be prepared for these situations and know how to handle them effectively.

- **Stay calm and collected:** When someone is trying to push your boundaries, it's important to stay calm and collected. Avoid getting defensive or reactive, as this can escalate the situation.

- **Reiterate your boundary:** If someone is ignoring your boundary, calmly and firmly restate it. For example, you might say, "I've already explained that I'm not comfortable with that, and I'm asking you to respect my decision."

- **Walk away if necessary:** If the situation becomes heated or you feel uncomfortable, it's okay to walk away. You are not obligated to engage in conversations that make you feel unsafe or disrespected.

- **Seek support:** If you are struggling to set boundaries on your own, it's okay to seek support from a trusted friend, family member, therapist, or coach. They can offer guidance and encouragement as you work on developing stronger boundaries.

The Benefits of Setting Boundaries

Setting boundaries may seem challenging, but the benefits are well worth the effort.

- **Improved mental and emotional health:** Boundaries protect your emotional well-being by shielding you from negative influences and stress. They help you create a safe space for yourself where you can feel comfortable and respected.

- **Stronger relationships:** Healthy boundaries actually improve relationships by fostering mutual respect and understanding. When you establish clear boundaries, you show others that you value yourself and that you expect the same respect from them.

- **Increased self-confidence:** Setting boundaries empowers you to take control of your life and make choices that align with your values and needs. This can lead to increased self-confidence and a sense of personal agency.

- **Reduced stress and conflict:** Clear boundaries help minimize conflict and misunderstandings. When everyone knows where the lines are, it becomes easier to navigate interactions and avoid unnecessary friction.

Setting Boundaries: A Continuous Journey

Setting boundaries is an ongoing process. It's not something you do once and then forget about. As you grow and evolve, your boundaries may change as well. It's important to be flexible and adaptable, willing to adjust your boundaries as needed to meet your evolving needs.

In Conclusion

Setting boundaries is an essential step in building strong and healthy relationships. It's about protecting your emotional well-being, creating a safe space for yourself, and communicating your needs effectively. By learning to set boundaries, you can empower yourself to live a more fulfilling and authentic life. Remember, you deserve to be respected and treated with care. Don't be afraid to stand up for yourself and create a life that is true to who you are.

Cultivating Empathy and Compassion

Empathy and compassion are the cornerstones of genuine connection, forming the bedrock upon which strong relationships are built. They are the bridges that span the chasm of individual experiences, allowing us to truly understand and appreciate the perspectives of others. Without empathy, our interactions become superficial, our judgments clouded by our own biases. With compassion, however, we open our hearts to the struggles and triumphs of those around us, fostering a sense of shared humanity that binds us together.

Imagine walking through a bustling city, your mind racing with thoughts and concerns. A homeless individual approaches you, asking for a few dollars. How do you respond? Do you ignore their plea, rushing past with a sense of indifference? Or do you pause, your heart aching for their situation? Do you offer a few coins, not just out of obligation, but from a genuine desire to alleviate their suffering?

This simple interaction highlights the power of empathy and compassion in everyday life. When we choose to see beyond our own immediate needs and connect with the experiences of others, we open ourselves up to a world of understanding and connection.

Empathy, at its core, is the ability to step into someone else's shoes, to understand their world from their perspective. It's not just about feeling sorry for someone, it's about truly grasping their feelings, their fears, their hopes, and their dreams. When we cultivate empathy, we begin to see the world through a broader lens, one that acknowledges the complexity of human experience.

Imagine a friend who is going through a difficult time, perhaps a job loss or a relationship breakdown. If we simply dismiss their pain, offering platitudes or focusing on our own worries, we miss an opportunity to truly connect. But if we take the time to listen, to understand their perspective, and to offer support without judgment, we can create a bond of understanding that strengthens the relationship.

Compassion, a close companion to empathy, is the feeling of concern for another person's suffering. It is the desire to help, to alleviate pain, and to ease hardship. Compassion doesn't require us to fix someone's problems, but rather to offer a gentle hand, a listening ear, and a reassuring presence.

Consider a loved one who is facing a chronic illness. Compassion doesn't mean we can magically cure them, but it does mean we can offer emotional support, practical assistance, and unwavering love. Compassion allows us to stand by their side, even in the darkest moments, offering a sense of hope and understanding.

In our interconnected world, where we are constantly bombarded with information and opinions, cultivating empathy and compassion is more important than ever. We are bombarded with information, often presented in a manner designed to trigger our fears and biases. This can lead to a world where we are quick to judge, to dismiss, and to create division.

However, by choosing to cultivate empathy and compassion, we can break down these barriers. We can engage in meaningful dialogue, listen with open hearts, and approach challenges with a spirit of cooperation rather than conflict. We can choose to see the humanity in others, even when their views differ from our own.

In the workplace, empathy and compassion are essential for building strong teams and fostering a positive and productive environment. When colleagues feel understood and respected, they are more likely to be engaged, motivated, and willing to collaborate. Empathy allows us to recognize the unique strengths and challenges of each team member, while compassion allows us to offer support and encouragement during times of stress or difficulty.

In our personal relationships, empathy and compassion are the glue that holds us together. When we understand and respect the perspectives of our loved ones, we create a foundation of trust, intimacy, and mutual support. Compassion allows us to forgive mistakes, to offer understanding during difficult times, and to nurture the bonds that make our relationships so precious.

Cultivating empathy and compassion isn't always easy. We live in a world that often rewards competitiveness, individualism, and self-interest. It can be tempting to retreat into our own worlds, to focus on our own needs and desires. However, the rewards of cultivating empathy and compassion are immeasurable.

Here are some practical tips for nurturing these essential qualities:

- **Practice Active Listening:** When interacting with others, make a conscious effort to listen attentively, without interrupting or formulating your response. Pay attention to both their verbal and nonverbal cues, and strive to understand their perspective.

- **Challenge Your Biases:** We all have biases, both conscious and unconscious. Take the time to reflect on your own beliefs and assumptions, and be open to challenging those that might limit your understanding of others.

- **Engage in Empathetic Dialogue:** Rather than engaging in debates or arguments, strive for a genuine dialogue where you seek to understand the other person's point of view. Ask questions, express curiosity, and avoid interrupting.

- **Practice Random Acts of Kindness:** Even small acts of kindness, such as holding a door for someone, offering a compliment, or simply being present for someone in need, can go a long way in fostering compassion.

- **Embrace Diversity:** Seek out opportunities to interact with people from diverse backgrounds, cultures, and experiences. Exposure to different perspectives can broaden your understanding of the world and cultivate empathy.

- **Engage in Compassionate Action:** Consider ways you can make a difference in the lives of others. Volunteering, donating to charities, or simply being a good neighbor can foster a sense of compassion and purpose.

- **Practice Self-Compassion:** Before you can truly extend compassion to others, you need to cultivate compassion for yourself. Practice self-forgiveness, acknowledge your limitations, and treat yourself with the same kindness and understanding you would offer to a loved one.

The journey of cultivating empathy and compassion is an ongoing one. It requires constant effort, self-reflection, and a willingness to embrace the complexity of human experience. However, the rewards of this journey are immense. By choosing to understand and connect with others, we create a world that is more compassionate, more understanding, and more filled with genuine connection.

Remember, the power of empathy and compassion lies not in simply feeling these emotions, but in actively embodying them in our interactions with the world. By making a conscious effort to cultivate these qualities, we not only enrich our own lives but also contribute to a more harmonious and fulfilling world for all.

Communicating Authentically

Imagine a world where you can express your thoughts and feelings with clarity and confidence, where you can truly connect with others on a deeper level, and where disagreements are resolved with respect and understanding. This world isn't a fantasy; it's a reality that can be cultivated through authentic communication.

Authentic communication is more than just words; it's about expressing yourself genuinely, listening attentively, and building trust through genuine interactions. It's the foundation of strong relationships, both personal and professional.

The Art of Clear Expression

Clear expression is the bridge between your thoughts and the world around you. It allows you to communicate your needs, ideas, and feelings effectively, ensuring that your message is received with clarity and understanding.

- **Honesty and Authenticity:** Begin by being true to yourself. Express your thoughts and feelings honestly, even if they're uncomfortable. This builds trust and fosters genuine connections.

- **Use "I" Statements:** Take ownership of your feelings and experiences. "I feel hurt when you..." is more effective than "You always make me feel..."

- **Choose Your Words Carefully:** Consider the impact of your words. Words have power, and choosing them thoughtfully can create positive and impactful communication.

- **Be Specific:** Avoid vagueness. Instead of saying "I'm stressed," try "I'm feeling overwhelmed by the deadline."

- **Non-Verbal Communication:** Your body language, tone of voice, and facial expressions speak volumes. Ensure they align with your spoken words for a consistent message.

The Power of Active Listening

Active listening is the foundation of understanding and empathy. It's not just about hearing the words someone says; it's about truly absorbing their message, both verbal and non-verbal.

- **Pay Attention:** Give the speaker your full focus. Put away distractions, maintain eye contact, and show genuine interest.

- **Listen Beyond the Words:** Observe their body language, tone, and facial expressions to gain a deeper understanding of their emotions and intentions.

- **Ask Questions:** Clarify their meaning with thoughtful questions. "Can you tell me more about...?" or "What do you mean by...?"

- **Summarize and Reflect:** Restate what you've heard to ensure understanding. "So, you're saying that..."

- **Avoid Interruptions:** Let the speaker finish their thoughts without jumping in with your own opinions or experiences.

Navigating Conflict Constructively

Conflicts are inevitable in any relationship. However, it's how we approach these conflicts that determines their outcome. Authentic communication plays a crucial role in resolving disagreements respectfully and finding common ground.

- **Choose the Right Time and Place:** Avoid discussing sensitive topics when either person is stressed, tired, or distracted. Choose a calm and private environment.

- **Focus on the Issue, Not the Person:** Address the specific issue at hand, avoiding personal attacks or blame.

- **Listen to Understand, Not to Respond:** Actively listen to your partner's perspective to gain a deeper understanding of their feelings and needs.

- **Find Common Ground:** Identify areas of agreement and work towards a solution that addresses both parties' concerns.

- **Stay Calm and Respectful:** Even when emotions run high, maintain composure and respect for each other.

Building Trust through Communication

Authentic communication is built on trust. It's about being reliable, honest, and open in your interactions. Here are some ways to cultivate trust:

- **Be Reliable:** Follow through on your promises and commitments.
- **Be Vulnerable:** Share your true thoughts and feelings, even if it makes you feel exposed. Vulnerability allows others to connect with you on a deeper level.
- **Respect Boundaries:** Acknowledge and respect the boundaries of others.
- **Apologize Sincerely:** When you make a mistake, take responsibility and apologize genuinely.

Examples and Exercises

- **Journaling:** Reflect on your communication style. What are your strengths? Where can you improve? Journaling can help you identify patterns and gain a deeper understanding of yourself.
- **Role-Playing:** Practice your communication skills in a safe environment. Role-play scenarios where you have to express your needs, ask for clarification, or resolve a conflict.
- **Active Listening Exercise:** Choose a friend or family member to practice active listening. Have them share a recent experience, and then summarize what you've heard back to them.

Beyond Words: The Power of Connection

Authentic communication goes beyond words; it's about creating a connection with the other person. It's about being present, showing genuine interest, and making the other person feel heard and valued.

- **Non-Verbal Communication:** Pay attention to your body language, tone of voice, and facial expressions. These nonverbal cues can enhance or hinder your message.

- **Empathy:** Try to understand the other person's perspective, even if you don't agree with them.
- **Emotional Intelligence:** Develop your emotional intelligence to understand and manage your own emotions and those of others.

The Journey of Authentic Communication

Mastering authentic communication is an ongoing journey. It requires practice, self-awareness, and a willingness to learn and grow. By embracing these principles, you can build stronger relationships, create deeper connections, and live a more fulfilling life.

Remember, authentic communication is a gift you give yourself and others. It's the foundation for building trust, understanding, and lasting connections. Embrace the power of authentic communication, and watch your relationships flourish.

Nurturing Your Relationships

Relationships are the lifeblood of our existence. They provide us with a sense of belonging, support, and love, enriching our lives in countless ways. However, like any garden, relationships require nurturing to flourish. Just as we need to water and care for plants to help them grow, we must actively cultivate our relationships to keep them healthy and strong.

Imagine a beautiful rose bush. At first, it might seem vibrant and full of life, but without proper care, it will eventually wither and die. The same applies to our relationships. Without nurturing, even the most promising connections can fade into the background.

So, how do we nurture our relationships and keep them thriving? The key is to invest in them, consistently and intentionally. Just as we make time for exercise, healthy eating, and other essential self-care practices, we need to carve out time for the people we care about. This doesn't mean we have to be constantly connected or spend hours on end together, but rather, we need to be present and engaged when we are with our loved ones.

There are countless ways to nurture our relationships, and each one is unique. However, some core principles can guide our efforts. Let's explore these principles:

1. Meaningful Interactions:

Meaningful interactions are the cornerstone of strong relationships. They are more than just casual conversations or fleeting exchanges. They involve truly connecting with another person, engaging in deep and meaningful dialogue, and sharing your thoughts, feelings, and experiences. These interactions can be as simple as a heartfelt conversation over coffee or a shared moment of laughter while watching a movie.

2. Acts of Kindness:

Kindness is a powerful force that strengthens bonds and fosters intimacy. Small gestures, like bringing a friend their favorite coffee or offering a helping hand when they are struggling, can go a long way in showing them you care. These acts of kindness don't have to be grand or extravagant; even the simplest gestures can have a profound impact on someone's life.

3. Expressing Appreciation:

Appreciation is the fuel that keeps relationships burning bright. When we express our gratitude for someone's presence, support, and kindness, we create a positive feedback loop that deepens our connection. A simple "thank you" or a heartfelt compliment can make a world of difference.

4. Quality Time:

In today's fast-paced world, it's easy to get caught up in the hustle and bustle of daily life and neglect our relationships. That's why it's crucial to make time for the people who matter most. Schedule regular date nights, family dinners, or coffee dates with friends to prioritize spending quality time together.

5. Active Listening:

True connection involves listening deeply to others. It means putting away our phones, silencing our internal chatter, and truly paying attention to what the other person is saying. When we listen actively, we show our loved ones that we value their thoughts and feelings and are genuinely interested in what they have to say.

6. Forgiveness:

Holding onto anger, resentment, or bitterness can poison a relationship and create distance. Forgiveness, while challenging, is an essential step towards healing and reconciliation. It doesn't mean forgetting or condoning wrongdoings but choosing to release the pain and negativity they bring.

7. Compromise and Flexibility:

Relationships are built on compromise and flexibility. No two people are exactly alike, so it's important to be willing to bend, adapt, and work together to find solutions that benefit both parties.

8. Respect and Trust:

Respect is the foundation of any healthy relationship. It involves valuing someone's thoughts, feelings, beliefs, and boundaries. Trust is built over time through consistent actions that demonstrate reliability, honesty, and loyalty.

Nurturing Relationships through Meaningful Interactions:

Meaningful interactions are the building blocks of strong relationships. They involve more than just casual conversation or fleeting exchanges. They are about creating a space for genuine connection and understanding. Here are some tips for engaging in meaningful interactions:

- **Be Present:** When you're with someone, put away your phone, silence your internal chatter, and truly engage with them. Give them your full attention and focus on what they're saying.

- **Ask Open-Ended Questions:** Instead of asking questions that can be answered with a simple "yes" or "no," ask open-ended questions that encourage deeper conversation and reflection. For example, instead of asking "How was your day?", ask "What was the highlight of your day?" or "What are you looking forward to this weekend?".

- **Share Your Thoughts and Feelings:** Vulnerability builds trust and intimacy. Share your thoughts and feelings with your loved ones, even if they're difficult or uncomfortable. Being open and honest creates a safe space for connection.

- **Listen Actively:** Active listening goes beyond just hearing the words someone is saying. It involves paying attention to their tone of voice, body language, and the emotions they're expressing. Reflect back what you hear to ensure you're understanding their message correctly.

- **Avoid Interrupting:** Allow the other person to finish their thoughts before you respond. Resist the urge to jump in with your own opinions or stories.

- **Find Common Ground:** Explore shared interests, experiences, or values to strengthen your connection. Even if you don't agree on everything, finding common ground can create a foundation for understanding and empathy.

- **Engage in Shared Activities:** Participating in activities you both enjoy, whether it's hiking, cooking, or playing a game, can create lasting memories and strengthen your bond.

- **Embrace Differences:** Recognize and appreciate the unique qualities of each person. Embrace your differences, as they add richness and complexity to your relationship.

- **Practice Gratitude:** Express your appreciation for the time you spend together and the positive impact they have on your life.

Nurturing Relationships through Acts of Kindness:

Acts of kindness are small gestures that can have a profound impact on our relationships. They show our loved ones that we care about them and are willing to go the extra mile to make them feel loved and appreciated. Here are some examples of acts of kindness that can nurture relationships:

- **Bring Them Their Favorite Treat:** A small gesture, like bringing a friend their favorite coffee or a colleague their favorite snack, can brighten their day and show them you're thinking of them.

- **Offer to Help with a Task:** If you know someone is struggling with a project, chore, or errand, offer to lend a helping hand. Even a small amount of help can make a big difference.

- **Send a Thoughtful Card or Note:** A handwritten card or note expressing your appreciation for someone's friendship or support can be a meaningful gesture.

- **Listen without Judgment:** If someone is going through a difficult time, be a supportive listener. Offer a shoulder to cry on and create a safe space for them to share their feelings without judgment.

- **Give a Compliment:** A heartfelt compliment can make someone's day. Recognize their efforts, strengths, or unique qualities and express your appreciation.

- **Do a Small Favor:** Offer to pick up groceries, walk their dog, or run an errand for them. Even a small favor can demonstrate your care and willingness to help.

- **Give the Gift of Time:** Offer to spend time with them, even if it's just for a few minutes. Quality time is a valuable gift.

- **Surprise Them with a Small Gift:** A small, thoughtful gift, like a book they've been wanting to read or a plant for their desk, can show them you're paying attention and care about their interests.

- **Be Present:** Being present in the moment with someone, putting away distractions and engaging in their conversation, is a powerful act of kindness.

Nurturing Relationships through Expressing Appreciation:

Appreciation is a powerful force that strengthens bonds and deepens connections. When we express our gratitude for someone's presence, support, and kindness, we create a positive feedback loop that nourishes the relationship. Here are some tips for expressing appreciation in your relationships:

- **Say "Thank You" Regularly:** Don't take your loved ones for granted. Express your appreciation for their presence in your life, their support during difficult times, and the joy they bring you.

- **Give Specific Compliments:** Instead of saying "You're great", be specific about what you appreciate. Tell them what they did, how it made you feel, and why it matters to you.

- **Acknowledge Their Efforts:** Recognize and appreciate their hard work, dedication, and commitment to their goals or relationships.

- **Show Your Appreciation Through Actions:** Actions speak louder than words. Show your loved ones you appreciate them by doing things for them, like cooking them dinner, planning a special outing, or offering to help with a task.

- **Write a Handwritten Letter:** A heartfelt letter expressing your gratitude and appreciation can be a lasting reminder of your feelings.

- **Share Your Appreciation with Others:** Spread the love by telling others how much you appreciate the people in your life.

By actively nurturing our relationships through meaningful interactions, acts of kindness, and expressing appreciation, we can cultivate deep and lasting connections that bring joy, meaning, and fulfillment to our lives. Remember, relationships are a two-way street. Be willing to give as much as you receive, and watch your relationships flourish!

CHAPTER 6

OVERCOMING OBSTACLES AND SETBACKS

Embracing Challenges as Growth Opportunities

Imagine a mountain climber, scaling a rugged peak. The path is treacherous, filled with rocky outcroppings, steep inclines, and unpredictable weather conditions. But this climber doesn't see these obstacles as insurmountable barriers; they view them as opportunities for growth, resilience, and personal triumph.

This is the mindset we need to cultivate in our own lives. Challenges, setbacks, and obstacles are inevitable parts of the human experience. They are not signs of failure or weakness; rather, they are opportunities for learning, growth, and transformation. Just like the mountain climber, we can choose to see these challenges as stepping stones on our journey towards becoming the best versions of ourselves.

The Power of Embracing Challenges

When we embrace challenges, we open ourselves up to a world of possibilities. We learn to adapt, to overcome adversity, and to develop a stronger sense of self. This process of facing and overcoming obstacles is what shapes us into the individuals we are meant to be.

Think about the challenges you've faced in your life – perhaps a difficult relationship, a career setback, a personal loss, or a health issue. These experiences, as painful as they may have been, likely taught you valuable lessons, strengthened your resolve, and helped you develop a deeper understanding of yourself and the world around you.

The Benefits of Overcoming Obstacles

Overcoming obstacles is not just about surviving; it's about thriving. It's about pushing beyond our comfort zones, developing resilience, and discovering hidden strengths we never knew we possessed.

Here are just a few of the many benefits of overcoming obstacles:

- **Increased Resilience:** Each challenge we overcome builds our resilience, making us better equipped to handle future difficulties. We learn to adapt, to bounce back, and to find strength in the face of adversity.

- **Personal Growth:** Challenges force us to confront our weaknesses, learn new skills, and develop a deeper understanding of ourselves. We grow as individuals through the process of facing and overcoming obstacles.

- **Self-Confidence:** Overcoming challenges boosts our self-confidence. We realize that we are capable of more than we ever thought possible, which empowers us to take on new challenges and achieve greater things in life.

- **Problem-Solving Skills:** Challenges require us to think creatively and develop problem-solving skills. We learn to analyze situations, identify solutions, and implement strategies that lead to successful outcomes.

- **Meaning and Purpose:** Overcoming challenges can give our lives a deeper sense of meaning and purpose. When we face adversity and emerge stronger, we gain a renewed appreciation for the value of life and the importance of striving for our goals.

Shifting Our Perspective

It's not always easy to embrace challenges, especially when we're in the midst of them. It's natural to feel overwhelmed, frustrated, or even defeated. But shifting our perspective can make a world of difference. Instead of viewing challenges as roadblocks, we can choose to see them as opportunities for growth and learning.

Here are a few strategies for shifting your perspective:

- **Reframe the Challenge:** Ask yourself, "What can I learn from this situation? How can I use this experience to grow?" By reframing the challenge, you shift your focus from the negativity to the potential for positive change.

- **Focus on the Positive:** Look for the silver lining in every challenge. Even in the darkest of times, there is always something to be grateful for, something positive to focus on.

- **Find the Lesson:** Every challenge contains a valuable lesson. Take the time to reflect on what went wrong, what you could have done differently, and what you can learn from the experience.

- **Seek Support:** Don't be afraid to reach out for help when you need it. Talk to a trusted friend, family member, therapist, or mentor. Having a support system can make a world of difference in navigating difficult times.

Building Resilience: The Key to Overcoming Obstacles

Resilience is the ability to bounce back from adversity and to adapt to change. It's the inner strength that allows us to persevere through difficult times and to emerge stronger on the other side.

Here are some strategies for building resilience:

- **Develop a Growth Mindset:** A growth mindset is the belief that our abilities are not fixed, but rather can be developed through effort, learning, and perseverance. When we embrace a growth mindset, we see challenges as opportunities for improvement and growth.

- **Practice Self-Compassion:** Be kind to yourself, especially during difficult times. Treat yourself with the same compassion and understanding that you would offer to a loved one.

- **Engage in Self-Care:** Take care of your physical and mental health. Get enough sleep, eat nutritious foods, exercise regularly, and engage in activities that bring you joy.

- **Practice Mindfulness:** Mindfulness involves paying attention to the present moment without judgment. By practicing mindfulness, you can develop a greater awareness of your thoughts, feelings, and sensations, which can help you manage stress and cultivate inner peace.

- **Connect with Others:** Building strong relationships with family, friends, and community members can provide a source of support, encouragement, and resilience.

The Power of Perseverance

Perseverance is the key to overcoming any obstacle. It's the ability to keep going, even when things are tough. It's about staying focused on our goals and refusing to give up, no matter the challenges we face.

Here are some strategies for cultivating perseverance:

- **Set Clear Goals:** Having clear goals provides a sense of direction and purpose. When we know what we are striving for, we are more likely to stay motivated and persevere.

- **Break Down Large Tasks:** Large tasks can seem overwhelming, so break them down into smaller, more manageable steps. This can make the journey feel less daunting and more achievable.

- **Celebrate Small Victories:** Don't underestimate the power of celebrating small victories. Acknowledging your progress, no matter how small, can boost your motivation and keep you moving forward.

- **Find Inspiration:** Surround yourself with people and resources that inspire you. Read books, listen to podcasts, watch movies, or attend events that motivate you to keep going.

- **Remember Your Why:** When you're feeling discouraged, remind yourself of your "why." Why are you pursuing this goal? What is the deeper purpose behind your efforts? Reconnecting with your purpose can give you the strength to persevere.

Learning from Failure

Failure is an inevitable part of life. We all make mistakes and experience setbacks. But the key is not to dwell on our failures but to learn from them and to use them as opportunities for growth.

Here are some tips for learning from failure:

- **Don't Be Afraid to Fail:** Failure is not the end of the world. It's an opportunity to learn, to adapt, and to grow. Embrace failure as a part of the learning process.

- **Analyze Your Mistakes:** Take the time to understand what went wrong. Identify your weaknesses, learn from your mistakes, and develop strategies to avoid making the same mistakes in the future.

- **Change Your Approach:** If your initial approach didn't work, try something different. Be flexible and willing to adjust your strategies as needed.

- **Seek Feedback:** Ask for feedback from others who can provide valuable insights into your performance and identify areas for improvement.

- **Don't Give Up:** Failure is not a reason to give up. It's a reason to try again, with a renewed determination to succeed.

The Role of Support Systems

We don't have to face life's challenges alone. Having a strong support system of friends, family, mentors, or even a therapist can make a world of difference in overcoming obstacles.

Here are some tips for building a supportive network:

- **Reach Out to Others:** Don't be afraid to reach out to those you trust for support. Let them know what you're going through and ask for help.

- **Be a Supportive Friend:** Offer support to others in need. Building strong relationships based on mutual support and understanding can help you navigate life's challenges.

- **Seek Professional Guidance:** If you're struggling with a particular challenge, don't hesitate to seek professional guidance. Therapists, coaches, and mentors can provide valuable support and tools for overcoming obstacles.

Finding Strength in Adversity

When we face adversity, we often discover hidden strengths we never knew we possessed. We realize that we are capable of more than we ever thought possible. This is the power of resilience – the ability to find strength within ourselves and to overcome any obstacle.

Here are some tips for finding strength in adversity:

- **Remember Your Past Successes:** Think about times you've faced challenges in the past and successfully overcome them. This can help you tap into your inner strength and remind yourself that you have the capacity to handle whatever comes your way.

- **Focus on What You Can Control:** There are many things in life that are beyond our control. Instead of dwelling on what we cannot change, focus on the things we can control, such as our thoughts, actions, and reactions.

- **Practice Gratitude:** Gratitude is a powerful tool for finding strength in adversity. When we focus on what we are grateful for, we shift our attention away from the negative and towards the positive.

- **Believe in Yourself:** Believe in your ability to overcome any challenge. Have faith in your own strength and resilience.

By embracing challenges, developing resilience, and finding strength in adversity, we can transform our lives and achieve extraordinary things. Remember, obstacles are not roadblocks; they are opportunities for growth and transformation. Choose to see them as stepping stones on your journey to becoming the best version of yourself.

The Power of Perseverance

Perseverance is the unwavering determination to keep going, even when faced with challenges, setbacks, and obstacles. It's the ability to rise above doubt, fear, and discouragement, and to continue pursuing your goals with relentless focus and commitment. Think of it as a powerful engine that drives you forward, propelling you towards your dreams, no matter the roadblocks you encounter.

Imagine a sculptor working on a masterpiece. They envision the final product, the beautiful form emerging from the raw material. But the process isn't easy. They chip away at the stone, dust fills the air, and their hands ache. They face frustrations, moments of doubt, and the temptation to give up. Yet, they persevere, driven by their vision and the conviction that their efforts will pay off. They know that every stroke, every chisel mark, is bringing them closer to their goal. And eventually, after countless hours of tireless dedication, the magnificent sculpture is revealed, a testament to their unwavering perseverance.

Perseverance is not about blindly pushing forward, ignoring warning signs, or refusing to adjust your course. It's about remaining flexible, adapting to changing circumstances, and constantly evaluating your approach. It's about learning from your mistakes, analyzing your strategies, and making course corrections when necessary. It's about being persistent but not stubborn, determined but not rigid.

Think of a marathon runner. They train rigorously, pushing themselves to the limit, knowing that the race will test their endurance. They're prepared for the physical and mental challenges, knowing that there will be moments of pain, fatigue, and self-doubt. Yet, they persevere, fueled by their desire to cross the finish line. They pace themselves, adjust their strategy, and push through every obstacle, drawing strength from their training and their commitment to their goal. And when they finally reach the finish line, they celebrate not only their victory but also the strength of their perseverance.

Here's a key principle: **Perseverance is a muscle you build over time**. It's a habit that takes practice, discipline, and a commitment to your goals. Like any muscle, it gets stronger with consistent exercise.

So how can you cultivate perseverance and turn it into a powerful force in your life? Here's a roadmap to navigate the path towards achieving your goals:

1. Set Clear and Achievable Goals:

Perseverance starts with a clear vision of what you want to achieve. Vague goals are like trying to navigate a maze without a map; it's easy to get lost and lose motivation. Set specific, measurable, achievable, relevant, and time-bound goals (SMART goals). This provides direction and clarity, making it easier to stay focused and motivated.

2. Break Down Goals into Smaller Steps:

Large, daunting goals can feel overwhelming. Break them down into smaller, manageable steps. Focus on conquering each small milestone, building momentum and confidence along the way. This makes the journey feel less daunting and provides a sense of accomplishment with each step. Think of it like building a staircase, where each step leads you higher, ultimately bringing you closer to your destination.

3. Embrace the Power of Visualization:

Imagine yourself achieving your goals. Visualize the process, the obstacles you might encounter, and the joy of success. This creates a mental blueprint, strengthening your resolve and helping you stay motivated, even during difficult times.

4. Find Your Why:

Why are you pursuing this goal? What motivates you? Connect to the deeper meaning behind your aspirations. When you're feeling discouraged, remind yourself of your purpose, your "why." This provides an internal source of fuel, driving you forward even when the road is tough.

5. Build a Supportive Network:

Surround yourself with people who believe in you, encourage you, and offer support. Their belief in your potential can be a powerful source of motivation.

6. Acknowledge and Celebrate Your Progress:

Celebrate your victories, no matter how small. Recognize your achievements, even if they seem insignificant. This reinforces your commitment and keeps you motivated.

7. Learn from Setbacks:

Don't let setbacks derail you. View them as opportunities to learn, adapt, and grow. Analyze what went wrong, make adjustments, and move forward with renewed determination.

8. Develop a Growth Mindset:

Believe in your ability to learn and grow. Challenge negative thoughts, embrace challenges as opportunities, and see failure as a stepping stone to success.

9. Develop a Resilience Plan:

Life is full of ups and downs. Develop a plan for dealing with challenges, setbacks, and disappointments. This could involve strategies like mindfulness, meditation, or simply taking a break to recharge.

10. Practice Self-Compassion:

Be kind to yourself, especially when facing challenges. Recognize that you are human, capable of making mistakes, and that setbacks are part of the journey. Offer yourself the same encouragement and support that you would give to a close friend.

11. Stay Persistent:

Perseverance is a marathon, not a sprint. There will be moments of doubt, fatigue, and temptation to give up. But keep going. Remember why you started, visualize your success, and never lose sight of your goals.

Perseverance is a potent force, capable of transforming dreams into reality. It's the key to overcoming obstacles, achieving your goals, and living a life filled with purpose, fulfillment, and satisfaction.

Learning from Failure

We all make mistakes. It's a part of being human. But what separates those who achieve greatness from those who remain stuck in their own struggles is the ability to learn from those mistakes. Failure isn't the end; it's a stepping stone. It's a chance to reflect, adjust, and emerge stronger.

Imagine a sculptor, meticulously chiseling away at a block of marble. Each stroke, each chip, is a learning experience. They study the form, feel the resistance, and learn from every misstep. They don't see those chips as wasted effort; they see them as vital pieces of the creative process, guiding them closer to their desired masterpiece.

This is the mindset we need to cultivate when facing setbacks. Instead of dwelling on the disappointment, we must embrace the opportunity to learn. Think of each stumble as a chance to reassess, to refine our approach, to gain valuable insights.

Consider the stories of the most successful individuals. They've all encountered failures along the way. J.K. Rowling's first Harry Potter manuscript was rejected by twelve publishers before finding a home. Walt Disney was fired from his newspaper job because he was told he "lacked imagination and had no good ideas." Steve Jobs was forced out of the company he founded, only to return years later and revolutionize the tech world.

These setbacks, these failures, didn't define them; they empowered them. They learned from their mistakes, adapted their strategies, and emerged stronger.

How do we learn from these inevitable bumps in the road? Here's a guide to help:

1. **Embrace a Growth Mindset:** We must first acknowledge that failure isn't a reflection of our worth, but an opportunity for growth. A growth mindset believes that abilities can be developed through effort and persistence. It sees challenges as opportunities to learn and improve.

2. **Reflect and Analyze:** Don't simply brush off setbacks as bad luck. Take the time to reflect. Analyze the situation. What went wrong? What could you have done differently? What insights did you gain from the experience?

3. **Identify Specific Lessons:** Don't just say, "I failed, and I learned something." Be specific. What are the concrete lessons you've learned? Did you need to improve your communication skills? Did you need to manage your time more effectively?

4. **Reframe Your Perspective:** Instead of viewing failure as a personal attack, reframe it as a valuable feedback loop. Think of it as a guide pointing you in the right direction.

5. **Create a Plan for Improvement:** Once you've identified the lessons, create a plan for improvement. What specific actions can you take to avoid similar mistakes in the future? Set clear goals, and take those steps, one at a time.

6. **Embrace Failure as a Teacher:** See failure as a friend, not a foe. It's there to guide you, to teach you, to push you further. Embrace it, learn from it, and allow it to propel you toward greater success.

7. **Learn from Others:** Seek out mentors, read biographies, or even listen to podcasts of successful individuals who have faced their own setbacks. Their stories can offer valuable insights and inspiration.

8. **Celebrate Your Resilience:** Don't forget to acknowledge your resilience in overcoming these obstacles. Give yourself credit for your ability to bounce back, to learn, and to grow.

Examples of Learning from Failure:

- **The Story of the Entrepreneur:** A young entrepreneur starts a new business with a groundbreaking idea. He pours his heart and soul into the project, working tirelessly for months. Unfortunately, the venture fails. He is devastated, feels like a failure, and is tempted to give up. But then, he takes a step back, reflects, and analyzes. He realizes that he failed to adequately market his product. He hadn't built strong relationships with potential customers. He didn't seek enough feedback. He takes these lessons to heart, and with renewed determination, he starts a new company, applying his newfound wisdom. This time, his business thrives.

- **The Student and the Exam:** A student studies hard for a big exam, confident in his understanding. He goes into the exam feeling prepared. However, he doesn't perform well and is disappointed with his score. Instead of letting the disappointment crush him, he analyzes his mistakes. He realizes he hadn't fully understood certain concepts. He also realizes he hadn't managed his time effectively during the exam. He uses this experience to improve his study strategies and time management skills. In the next exam, he excels.

Learning from Failure: A Journey of Growth

The journey of learning from failure is not always easy. It requires courage, resilience, and a willingness to embrace imperfection. But by embracing setbacks as opportunities for growth, we unlock our potential for continuous improvement.

Imagine a river carving its way through a mountain. It doesn't avoid the rocks and obstacles; it encounters them, it navigates around them, it sometimes even crashes against them. But through this relentless journey, the river carves a deeper channel, becoming stronger, more powerful, and more beautiful.

We, too, can learn from every obstacle, every challenge, every stumble. Like the river, we can use those experiences to shape us, to mold us, to make us more resilient, more capable, and more fulfilled.

So, the next time you face a setback, remember the sculptor, the entrepreneur, the student. Remember that failure is not the end; it's a turning point, a chance to learn, to adapt, and to emerge stronger. Embrace the journey, and let each stumble guide you towards your own masterpiece.

The Role of Support Systems

Imagine a mountain climber scaling a treacherous peak. The wind howls, the snow falls, and the path is narrow and unforgiving. The climber, though strong and determined, might stumble and fall, losing their footing. They might even feel tempted to give up and turn back. But what if, at that crucial moment, a supportive hand reached out to help them regain their balance and keep going? This is the power of a strong support system.

Just as a climber benefits from the support of a trusted guide and fellow climbers, we too can navigate life's challenges with greater ease and resilience when we have people we can lean on. Building a strong support system is essential for overcoming obstacles, bouncing back from setbacks, and ultimately achieving our goals.

Think of your support system as a safety net, a group of people who believe in you, encourage you, and offer guidance and support when you need it most. This network might include close friends, family members, mentors, or even a therapist or counselor. Each person brings a unique perspective, a different kind of support that can help you grow and thrive.

Friends: The Cheerleaders of Life

Friends play a crucial role in our support system. They are the ones who celebrate our victories, offer a listening ear during difficult times, and provide a shoulder to cry on when we need it most. True friends offer unconditional love, acceptance, and encouragement, even when we make mistakes or experience setbacks. They help us maintain a positive outlook, reminding us of our strengths and encouraging us to keep moving forward.

Think of your friends as your cheerleaders, your personal pep squad, cheering you on from the sidelines. They offer words of affirmation, celebrate your accomplishments, and help you stay motivated, even when the going gets tough. Their belief in you becomes your own, bolstering your confidence and resilience.

Family: The Unwavering Foundation

Family, regardless of its structure or composition, serves as a foundation, a bedrock of unconditional love and support. Family members are often our first and most enduring source of strength and stability. They have seen us through thick and thin, they know our history, and they hold a special place in our hearts.

While family members may not always be the perfect source of guidance or advice, they are often our most reliable source of love and acceptance. They offer a sense of belonging, a place where we can be ourselves without judgment. Their support can be invaluable during times of crisis or uncertainty, providing a safe haven where we can recharge and rebuild.

Mentors: The Guiding Lights

Mentors are invaluable members of our support system. They are individuals who have experience, wisdom, and a genuine desire to help us grow and succeed. They can be teachers, coaches, colleagues, or even friends who have gone before us and have insights into the path we are taking.

Mentors offer guidance, advice, and support, helping us navigate challenges, make informed decisions, and develop our skills. They can provide valuable feedback, challenge our assumptions, and push us to reach our full potential. Their experience and wisdom serve as a guiding light, illuminating our path and helping us avoid pitfalls.

The Power of Seeking Support

It's important to remember that asking for help is not a sign of weakness, but rather a sign of strength and self-awareness. We all need support at times, and there is no shame in reaching out to those who care about us. In fact, the more we reach out, the stronger our support system becomes.

Building a Strong Support System

Building a strong support system is an ongoing process. It requires effort, intentionality, and a willingness to be open and vulnerable. Here are some tips:

- **Be a Supportive Friend:** If you want others to support you, be a supportive friend to others. Be present, listen attentively, offer encouragement, and celebrate their victories.

- **Nurture Your Family Ties:** Make an effort to stay connected with family members, even if they live far away. Reach out regularly, share your experiences, and show them that you care.

- **Seek Out Mentors:** Look for individuals who inspire you, who have achieved what you aspire to, and who are willing to share their knowledge and experience. Be proactive in connecting with potential mentors and expressing your desire to learn from them.

- **Join a Support Group:** Consider joining a support group related to a challenge you are facing, such as a grief support group or a weight loss support group. These groups provide a safe space to share your experiences, connect with others who understand, and receive support from people who have been through similar challenges.

- **Reach Out to Professionals:** If you are struggling with a significant challenge, consider seeking professional support from a therapist, counselor, or coach. These professionals can provide guidance, tools, and strategies for navigating your specific difficulties.

- **Engage in Activities You Enjoy:** Engaging in activities that you enjoy can help you connect with like-minded people who share your interests. This can lead to new friendships, connections, and a sense of belonging.

- **Be Vulnerable and Open:** Sharing your thoughts, feelings, and challenges with others can help you build deeper connections and receive the support you need. Be willing to be vulnerable and open with those you trust.

The Benefits of a Strong Support System

The benefits of having a strong support system are numerous. A strong support system can help you:

- **Overcome Challenges:** Challenges are a part of life. When we face difficulties, having people we can lean on can make the journey less daunting. Their encouragement, advice, and support can help us stay motivated, find solutions, and overcome obstacles.

- **Bounce Back from Setbacks:** Setbacks are inevitable. We all experience failures, disappointments, and setbacks along the way. Having a strong support system can help us recover from these experiences, learn from our mistakes, and move forward with renewed determination.

- **Maintain a Positive Outlook:** It's easy to get bogged down by negativity. Surrounding yourself with positive people can help you maintain a more positive outlook and focus on the good in life. Their optimism can inspire you and help you see things from a different perspective.

- **Improve Your Physical and Mental Health:** Strong social connections have been linked to better physical and mental health. People with strong support systems tend to experience less stress, depression, and anxiety. They are more likely to engage in healthy behaviors, such as exercise and eating a healthy diet, and are better able to cope with life's challenges.

- **Achieve Your Goals:** Having a strong support system can help you set and achieve your goals. Their encouragement, feedback, and accountability can help you stay motivated, focused, and on track.

The Takeaway

Building a strong support system is an investment in your well-being. It's an essential part of living a fulfilling and meaningful life. By nurturing your relationships, seeking out mentors, and reaching out when you need help, you can create a network of support that will help you navigate life's challenges, overcome obstacles, and achieve your full potential. Remember, you are not alone on this journey. Surround yourself with people who care about you and who believe in your dreams. With a strong support system by your side, you can achieve anything you set your mind to.

Finding Strength in Adversity

The human spirit possesses an incredible capacity to endure and triumph over adversity. It's in the face of hardship, the moments that test our very core, that we discover hidden reservoirs of strength and resilience we never knew we had. It's like a dormant muscle, waiting for the right moment to flex its power.

Think about the stories of those who have overcome seemingly insurmountable obstacles. Nelson Mandela spent decades in prison for his fight against apartheid, yet emerged as a symbol of hope and forgiveness. Oprah Winfrey, a victim of childhood trauma and abuse, rose to become a media mogul and global icon. Their experiences, while unique, hold a common thread – the refusal to succumb to despair, the unwavering belief in their own ability to create a better future.

This doesn't mean that every setback is a stepping stone to greatness. It's not about romanticizing suffering, but about recognizing the inherent human ability to adapt, learn, and grow in the face of challenges. It's about embracing the uncomfortable truth that adversity is an inevitable part of life, and that our response to it defines who we are.

Finding strength in adversity starts with a shift in mindset. Instead of viewing challenges as insurmountable obstacles, reframe them as opportunities for growth and learning. When we embrace the possibility that difficult experiences can lead to greater understanding and personal evolution, our response shifts from fear and avoidance to curiosity and acceptance. We start to see the challenge not as a threat, but as a catalyst for transformation.

This shift requires a conscious effort to move away from the automatic negative thought patterns that often emerge in the face of adversity. We are wired to focus on the threat, to magnify the potential for harm and minimize our own capacity to cope. However, with practice, we can learn to challenge these thought patterns and replace them with more empowering ones.

This process starts with self-awareness. Pay attention to your thoughts and feelings when faced with a challenge. Recognize the negative thoughts that arise, such as "I can't handle this," or "I'm going to fail." Once you identify these thoughts, you can start to question their validity. Ask yourself: "Is this thought truly helpful? Is it based on evidence, or on fear and assumptions? What would a more supportive and encouraging voice tell me?"

By challenging your negative thoughts, you can begin to create space for a more positive and empowering perspective. Instead of focusing on the threat, start to consider the potential for learning, growth, and even opportunity. Remind yourself that you have faced challenges before and emerged stronger. You have the inner resources to navigate this situation, and you can learn valuable lessons from the process.

But finding strength in adversity doesn't happen in isolation. It's crucial to build a supportive network of people who can offer encouragement, guidance, and a listening ear. Surround yourself with friends, family, mentors, or community members who believe in your ability to overcome challenges. Share your struggles, ask for support, and allow yourself to be vulnerable.

Sometimes, simply talking about what you're going through can help you gain clarity and perspective. A supportive friend can offer a different viewpoint, challenge your negative assumptions, and remind you of your strengths. They can help you see the situation from a more objective perspective and encourage you to take action towards a more positive outcome.

Finding strength in adversity is a journey, not a destination. There will be moments of doubt, fear, and frustration. It's important to be kind to yourself during these times and remember that you are not alone. Every human being experiences setbacks and challenges; it's part of the human experience. But it's how we choose to respond that shapes our character and determines our ultimate resilience.

Remember, you are capable of extraordinary things. You have the strength within you to overcome any obstacle, to learn from your experiences, and to emerge from adversity as a more resilient and capable person. Believe in yourself, embrace the challenges, and remember that every setback is an opportunity for growth and transformation.

CHAPTER 7

DISCOVERING YOUR PURPOSE

The Search for Meaning

The search for meaning is a fundamental human desire, a quest that has captivated philosophers, poets, and everyday people for centuries. It's about finding a sense of purpose, a reason for being, that gives our lives significance and direction. It's the driving force behind our deepest aspirations, our dreams, and our actions.

Imagine a life without purpose, a life devoid of meaning. It would be like a ship adrift at sea, aimlessly tossed about by the currents of uncertainty. It would be a life lacking direction, a life devoid of a compass to guide us toward our true north.

But finding meaning isn't a destination, it's a journey. It's not a singular event that happens overnight; it's a process of self-discovery that unfolds over time. And it's a journey that can be both exhilarating and challenging.

For some, the search for meaning begins with a profound realization, a moment of clarity that illuminates the path ahead. It might be triggered by a life-changing event, a personal crisis, or a simple yet profound reflection. It might be a sudden awakening to a previously unrealized passion, a hidden talent, or a deep-seated desire to make a difference in the world.

For others, the journey is more gradual. It's a slow, steady process of exploration, trial, and error. It's about experimenting with different roles, experiences, and paths, seeking out what resonates with our deepest values and aspirations. It's about embracing our passions, pursuing our dreams, and discovering what brings us true joy and fulfillment.

The meaning we find in life is deeply personal. It's not a one-size-fits-all answer, but a unique tapestry woven from our experiences, values, and aspirations. It's about aligning our actions with what matters most to us, finding ways to contribute to the world, and creating a life that reflects our true selves.

There are countless ways to discover your purpose. Here are some approaches that have proven to be effective:

1. Reflecting on Your Values:

Begin by exploring your core values. What principles guide your decisions? What is important to you in life? Take time to journal, meditate, or engage in quiet reflection. Ask yourself questions like:

What do I believe in?
What are my deepest convictions?
What do I stand for?
What brings me true joy and satisfaction?

Your values will act as a compass, guiding you towards a life that is aligned with your true self.

2. Identifying Your Passions:

Passions are powerful motivators, driving us to pursue our dreams with enthusiasm and dedication. Explore what truly interests you, what makes your heart sing, and what you would do even if you weren't paid for it. Ask yourself:

What do I enjoy doing in my free time?
What activities bring me a sense of flow and deep engagement?
What makes me feel truly alive?

Your passions are clues to your purpose, leading you to activities that bring both meaning and fulfillment.

3. Exploring Your Strengths and Talents:

Take an inventory of your strengths and talents. What are you naturally good at? What do you excel in? What do others compliment you on? Understanding your inherent abilities will help you identify areas where you can contribute and shine.

4. Embracing Your Curiosity:

Curiosity is a gateway to discovery. Be open to new experiences, explore different fields, and ask questions. Embrace the unknown and challenge your assumptions. You never know where you'll find inspiration and uncover a hidden talent or passion.

5. Seeking Mentors and Guidance:

Don't be afraid to seek guidance from others who have found meaning in their lives. Connect with mentors, coaches, or people you admire. They can share their experiences, offer advice, and inspire you on your journey of self-discovery.

6. Experimenting with Different Roles and Experiences:

Don't be afraid to try new things and step outside of your comfort zone. Volunteer, take on a new hobby, explore different career paths, and engage in activities that challenge you and expand your horizons.

7. Reflecting on Your Experiences:

As you navigate your journey of self-discovery, take time to reflect on your experiences. What have you learned? What insights have you gained? What lessons have resonated with you? The reflections will help you clarify your purpose and refine your path.

8. Embracing Your Unique Journey:

Remember that your path is unique. Don't compare yourself to others. Embrace your individuality and celebrate the journey of discovering your purpose.

What Does Meaning Mean to You?

The meaning you find in life will be unique to your experiences, values, and aspirations. For some, it might be about making a tangible impact on the world, perhaps through philanthropy, activism, or scientific breakthroughs. For others, it might be about cultivating deep connections with loved ones, nurturing their personal growth, and creating a loving and supportive family.

Meaning can also be found in artistic expression, intellectual pursuits, or simply appreciating the beauty and wonder of the world around us. It's about finding what brings you joy, fulfillment, and a sense of purpose.

The Benefits of Finding Meaning:

Living a life with purpose offers numerous benefits:

- **Increased Happiness and Fulfillment:** When we align our actions with our values and passions, we experience a sense of deep satisfaction and fulfillment.

- **Enhanced Motivation and Drive:** Having a sense of purpose provides a powerful motivator, propelling us to pursue our goals with enthusiasm and determination.

- **Improved Well-being:** Living a purpose-driven life is associated with better mental and physical health, as it fosters a sense of meaning and connection.

- **Increased Resilience and Adaptability:** When we have a clear sense of purpose, we're better able to navigate challenges and setbacks. We know what matters most to us, and we're more resilient in the face of adversity.

Remember, finding meaning is an ongoing journey. It's not a one-time event, but a continuous process of exploration, reflection, and growth. Embrace the journey, be patient with yourself, and allow your purpose to unfold organically. You are on your own unique path, and the journey itself is a testament to the meaning you bring to the world.

Connecting Your Values and Passions

Imagine your life as a canvas, vast and awaiting a masterpiece. Now, imagine those vibrant colors, those strokes of brilliance that bring the painting to life – those are your values and passions. They are the essence of who you are, the driving forces behind your desires, and the compass that guides you towards a life of fulfillment.

This journey of self-discovery is a personal quest, a treasure hunt within your own heart. The first step is to understand what truly matters to you. What are your core values? These are the fundamental beliefs that guide your actions and decisions. They shape your perspective on life, your relationships, and your choices. Perhaps you value honesty, integrity, compassion, or creativity.

Next, explore your passions. Passions are those activities that ignite a fire within you, that make you feel alive and energized. They are the things you would do even if you weren't paid, even if you didn't have to. Do you have a passion for music, art, writing, helping others, or learning new things?

Now comes the magic: aligning your values and passions. This is where the true beauty unfolds. Imagine a life where your actions are guided by your deepest beliefs and your days are filled with activities that light you up from within. This is the path to a life of purpose and fulfillment.

Take time to reflect on your core values. Journal about them, discuss them with a trusted friend or mentor, or simply contemplate them in the stillness of your heart. Ask yourself questions like:

What is most important to me in life?
What are the qualities I admire in others?
What principles do I strive to live by?
What are my non-negotiables?

Once you have a clear understanding of your values, turn your attention to your passions. Allow yourself to explore different interests, try new things, and listen to your heart.

What activities make you feel most energized and alive?

What do you find yourself gravitating towards?
What do you dream about doing?
What makes you lose track of time?

As you identify your values and passions, start noticing the connections between them. Are there themes that emerge? Do your values inform your passions? For example, if you value creativity and you are passionate about writing, these two elements come together to form a powerful force guiding you towards a fulfilling life.

It's important to note that your values and passions may evolve over time. You might discover new values or passions, or you might re-prioritize those you already hold. That's perfectly natural! The key is to stay open and curious, to embrace the journey of self-discovery and allow your values and passions to guide you.

When you align your actions with your values and passions, you create a life that is authentically yours. You move from a sense of emptiness or dissatisfaction to a state of purpose, joy, and fulfillment.

Consider this example: Imagine someone who values family, connection, and making a difference in the world. They may have a passion for cooking and enjoy bringing people together for meals. This individual might choose to use their passion for cooking to create a catering business that supports a local charity or to start a community garden that brings neighbors together. In this scenario, their actions are aligned with their values and passions, leading to a life of purpose and fulfillment.

The beauty of aligning your values and passions lies in the sense of purpose and meaning it brings. It's about living in alignment with your true self, making choices that resonate with your deepest beliefs, and pursuing activities that spark joy and excitement.

When you live a life guided by your values and passions, you are not only fulfilling your own potential but also contributing to the world in a meaningful way. You are living a life that is truly yours, a life that shines bright and inspires others to do the same.

As you embark on this journey, remember that there is no right or wrong way to do this. The process is personal, unique to you, and ever evolving. Be patient with yourself, be kind to yourself, and allow yourself to explore, experiment, and discover the beauty that lies within you.

Remember, this is not just about finding your purpose; it's about creating a life that is authentically yours, a life that is filled with meaning, joy, and the vibrant colors of your true self.

So, take a deep breath, open your heart, and embrace the journey of connecting your values and passions. The path to a fulfilling life awaits.

The Power of Contribution

The very essence of our being yearns to make a difference, to leave a positive imprint on the world around us. This inherent desire to contribute is not merely a noble aspiration, but a fundamental aspect of our human nature. It is the driving force behind countless acts of kindness, creativity, and innovation that have shaped the course of history.

Imagine a world devoid of contributions, a world where each individual lived solely for themselves, without a thought for the well-being of others. Such a world would lack the spark of compassion, the surge of creativity, and the collective spirit that drive progress and upliftment. It is through our contributions, however small or grand they may be, that we weave the fabric of a better, more harmonious society.

Contribution transcends the realm of grand gestures and philanthropic endeavors. It manifests in the smallest acts of kindness, in the unwavering dedication to our work, in the passion we bring to our pursuits, and in the unwavering commitment to personal growth. It is the sum total of these seemingly insignificant moments that create a ripple effect, spreading outwards to touch the lives of those around us.

The power of contribution lies in its ability to ignite a chain reaction, inspiring others to follow suit. When we see someone going above and beyond, giving selflessly, or striving for excellence, it stirs within us a yearning to emulate their example. It prompts us to ask ourselves, "What can I do to make a difference?"

There are countless ways to contribute to society, each tailored to our unique talents, passions, and circumstances. Whether it's volunteering our time, donating to a cause we believe in, mentoring others, or simply extending a helping hand to those in need, every act of contribution, however small, carries immense weight.

Let's explore some avenues for making a positive impact:

Volunteering:

Volunteering is a powerful way to connect with our community and make a tangible difference. It allows us to utilize our skills and talents to address social issues, enhance the well-being of others, and create a more just and equitable society. From working with underprivileged children to assisting seniors, volunteering offers a wide range of opportunities to give back and make a meaningful contribution.

Mentoring:

Mentorship is a transformative process that fosters personal and professional growth by providing guidance, support, and encouragement. Whether we mentor a young professional, a student, or even a friend, we can play a vital role in shaping their lives and empowering them to reach their full potential. By sharing our knowledge, experience, and insights, we not only help others but also deepen our own understanding and strengthen our own resolve.

Supporting Charities and Non-Profit Organizations:

Supporting charities and non-profit organizations allows us to contribute to causes we believe in, whether it's environmental protection, poverty alleviation, or healthcare. Our financial support can help these organizations make a tangible difference in the lives of countless individuals, addressing critical issues and fostering positive change.

Advocacy and Activism:

Advocating for social justice and raising awareness about important issues can make a significant difference. By speaking up for what we believe in, participating in peaceful protests, or supporting organizations working to bring about change, we can contribute to creating a more equitable and just society.

Inspiring Others:

Perhaps the most impactful way to contribute is by inspiring others through our actions, words, and attitudes. When we live authentically, pursue our passions, and strive for excellence, we serve as role models for others. Our positive energy, unwavering commitment, and infectious enthusiasm can motivate those around us to embark on their own journeys of self-discovery and personal growth.

The power of contribution lies not only in the tangible impact we make but also in the transformative effect it has on our own lives. When we dedicate ourselves to making a difference, we unlock a wellspring of joy, purpose, and fulfillment. We discover that our own happiness is intrinsically intertwined with the well-being of others.

As we embrace the power of contribution, we transcend the boundaries of our individual selves and connect with something greater than ourselves. We become part of a collective effort, working towards a shared vision of a better future for all. And in this journey of giving, we discover a profound sense of purpose, meaning, and fulfillment that enriches our lives in ways we could never have imagined.

Remember, every act of contribution, however small, has the power to make a difference. Embrace the opportunity to contribute to the world around you and experience the joy of making a positive impact. You have the power to change the world, one act of kindness, one moment of inspiration, and one step at a time.

Embracing Your Unique Contribution

Imagine you have a unique, vibrant piece of art, a painting, a sculpture, a musical composition that holds a special significance. It's not just about the beauty or the skill involved; it's about the message, the story it tells, the emotions it evokes. It's about your unique contribution to the world.

That's what your purpose is, your unique contribution to the world. It's not about finding a grand mission or a life-altering cause, but about discovering your own talents and passions and finding ways to share them with others. It's about using your gifts to make a difference, even in small ways.

Finding your purpose isn't about becoming a famous artist or a groundbreaking scientist. It's about embracing the everyday opportunities to contribute, to make a positive impact on your community, your loved ones, and even the world at large.

Think about your unique skillset, your strengths, your talents, and your passions. Maybe you're a gifted storyteller, a compassionate listener, a creative problem solver, or a skilled musician.

Consider how you can use your gifts to make a difference in the lives of others. Can you volunteer your time at a local soup kitchen, mentor a young person, share your knowledge through teaching or writing, or simply offer a kind word and a listening ear?

Sometimes, the smallest acts of kindness can have the biggest impact.

Perhaps you're an excellent cook. Share your recipes and create a community meal for your neighbors. Perhaps you're skilled at gardening. Share your knowledge and expertise by creating a community garden or volunteering at a local farm. Perhaps you're an artist with a passion for beauty. Offer to paint murals or create art installations to brighten up your community.

Maybe you're a tech enthusiast. Share your skills by teaching seniors how to use computers or setting up a free tech support hotline for those who need it. Maybe you're a musician. Offer to perform at local nursing homes or organize free community concerts. Maybe you're a writer. Share your stories and insights by writing for local newspapers or creating a blog.

Your contribution might not be monumental or world-changing, but it can still be meaningful and impactful. It's about finding ways to use your unique gifts to make a difference in the lives of others, however big or small.

Remember, you have something special to offer the world. Don't underestimate your unique talents and the positive impact you can have. Your purpose is waiting to be discovered, and it's often found in the simplest acts of generosity, compassion, and creativity.

Here are some practical steps to help you identify and embrace your unique contribution:

1. Reflect on Your Passions:

- **Take a quiet moment to reflect.** Close your eyes, take a few deep breaths, and let your mind wander. Think about the things that bring you joy, the activities that make you feel truly alive.
- **Create a list.** Jot down everything that comes to mind, no matter how small or insignificant it may seem.
- **Analyze your list.** Look for patterns and common themes. What are the underlying values or passions that seem to emerge?

2. Identify Your Strengths and Talents:

- **Think about your accomplishments.** What are you good at? What skills have you developed over the years?
- **Ask for feedback.** Talk to friends, family, colleagues, or mentors and ask them what they believe your strengths are.
- **Don't be afraid to be honest with yourself.** Identify your skills and talents, even if you haven't had a chance to use them in a professional setting.

3. Explore Your Interests and Values:

- **Think about the things you enjoy learning about.** What topics fascinate you?
- **Consider your personal values.** What principles are most important to you?

- **Connect your interests and values to your skills.** How can you use your talents to make a difference in areas that align with your passions and values?

4. Seek Inspiration from Others:

- **Look to role models.** Who inspires you? What are their stories, and how have they made a difference in the world?
- **Read books and articles.** Explore stories about people who are making a positive impact in their communities and the world.
- **Network and connect with others.** Seek out mentors, friends, or colleagues who are passionate about making a difference.

5. Start Small and Be Patient:

- **Don't overthink it.** It's okay to start with small, manageable actions.
- **Don't be afraid to experiment.** Try different activities, volunteer in different organizations, and explore different ways to use your talents.
- **Be patient with yourself.** Finding your purpose is a journey, not a destination.

Remember, your purpose is not something to be found, it's something to be created. It's about using your unique gifts and talents to make a positive impact in the world. It's about discovering your own unique way to contribute, no matter how big or small.

As you embark on this journey of self-discovery and purpose, remember these key principles:

- **Be Kind to Yourself:** Be patient and compassionate with yourself as you navigate this process. It's a journey, not a race.

- **Embrace Your Uniqueness:** Celebrate your unique talents, quirks, and perspectives. You have something special to offer the world.
- **Don't Be Afraid to Be Yourself:** Be authentic and true to yourself. The world needs your unique voice and contribution.
- **Stay Curious and Open-Minded:** Be willing to explore new interests, learn new skills, and challenge your own beliefs.
- **Connect with Others:** Build meaningful relationships with people who share your values and passions.
- **Give Back:** Find ways to contribute to your community and make a difference in the lives of others.

As you explore your passions, identify your strengths, and embrace your unique contribution, you'll discover a profound sense of fulfillment and purpose. You'll realize that you don't need to change the world; you just need to use your talents to make it a better place, one small act of kindness, one creative expression, one meaningful contribution at a time.

Living a Purposeful Life

Imagine a life where your actions are aligned with your deepest values, where your passions fuel your every step, and where each day brings a sense of purpose and fulfillment. This is the essence of living a purpose-driven life, a life that resonates with authenticity and joy.

Think of it like a ship sailing on a vast ocean. Without a compass or a clear destination, the ship might drift aimlessly, tossed about by the winds and currents of life's uncertainties. But with a defined purpose, a guiding star, the ship can navigate with confidence, knowing exactly where it's headed.

A purpose-driven life is like having that guiding star, a clear sense of direction that illuminates your path and empowers you to navigate life's challenges with resilience and purpose. It's about aligning your actions with your values, living in accordance with your deepest beliefs, and pursuing activities that bring you joy and fulfillment.

The benefits of living a purpose-driven life are manifold, enriching your life in ways you may not have even imagined.

- **The Power of Inner Harmony:** When you live in alignment with your values and passions, you experience a profound sense of inner harmony. Your actions and beliefs become congruent, creating a sense of peace and coherence that permeates every aspect of your life. This inner harmony fosters a feeling of alignment, reducing internal conflict and allowing you to move through the world with greater clarity and purpose.

- **Unleashing Your Potential:** Purpose acts as a powerful catalyst, igniting your innate potential and pushing you to strive for greatness. When you're driven by a compelling purpose, you tap into a wellspring of motivation and determination, pushing your limits and achieving things you never thought possible. This sense of purpose fuels your creativity, inspires you to learn and grow, and empowers you to achieve extraordinary things.

- **Greater Happiness and Fulfillment:** Living a purpose-driven life brings a deep sense of fulfillment and happiness that goes beyond fleeting pleasures. It's a happiness that stems from knowing your worth, contributing to something meaningful, and making a difference in the world. This profound sense of purpose fuels your inner fire, giving you a sense of meaning and satisfaction that is truly transformative.

- **Resilience in the Face of Challenges:** When life throws unexpected challenges your way, a strong sense of purpose acts as an anchor, grounding you and providing the strength to persevere. Knowing your "why" allows you to navigate adversity with resilience and a steadfast belief in your ability to overcome obstacles.

- **Increased Self-Awareness:** Embracing a purpose-driven life requires introspection and self-awareness. You become more attuned to your values, passions, and desires. This journey of self-discovery deepens your understanding of yourself, leading to greater self-acceptance and a more authentic expression of who you truly are.

- **The Power of Contribution:** A purpose-driven life often involves making a contribution to something bigger than yourself. This could be contributing to your community, pursuing your passions, or leaving a legacy that will benefit generations to come. This sense of contribution gives you a feeling of meaning and purpose, knowing that your actions have a positive impact on the world around you.

- **Connecting with Your Authentic Self:** When you align your actions with your values and passions, you connect with your authentic self, living a life that is true to your core beliefs and aspirations. This authenticity brings a sense of freedom and liberation, allowing you to express yourself freely and authentically.

A Life of Purpose: A Journey of Discovery

Discovering your purpose is not a destination, but a journey. It's an ongoing process of introspection, exploration, and self-discovery. There is no single blueprint for finding purpose, as it's unique to each individual. However, there are certain principles and practices that can guide you on this transformative journey.

Here are some powerful steps you can take to embrace a purpose-driven life:

1. Self-Reflection and Introspection:

- **Identify your values:** Take some time to reflect on the core principles that guide your life. What do you believe in? What is important to you? What values shape your decisions?
- **Explore your passions:** What activities light you up? What do you enjoy doing, even if you don't get paid for it? What are you naturally drawn to?
- **Journaling and Reflection:** Keep a journal to record your thoughts, feelings, and insights. Use this space to reflect on your values, passions, and dreams.

2. Connect with Your Authentic Self:

- **Identify your strengths and talents:** What are you good at? What skills do you possess? What natural abilities do you have?
- **Embrace your individuality:** Celebrate your uniqueness and your unique contribution to the world. Don't compare yourself to others, but rather embrace your own path.
- **Release limiting beliefs:** Examine any negative self-talk or limiting beliefs that hold you back. Challenge these beliefs and replace them with positive affirmations that support your growth and aspirations.

3. Define Your Purpose:

- **Ask yourself powerful questions:** What legacy do you want to leave behind? What impact do you want to have on the world? What kind of difference do you want to make?

- **Imagine your ideal life:** What would your ideal life look like? What would you be doing? What would your days be like?

- **Visualize your future:** Use visualization techniques to imagine yourself living a life aligned with your purpose.

4. Take Action:

- **Start small:** Don't try to change everything at once. Start with small, achievable steps that align with your purpose.

- **Embrace opportunities:** Be open to new experiences and opportunities that align with your values and passions.

- **Don't be afraid to fail:** Failure is a natural part of the journey. Embrace setbacks as opportunities for learning and growth.

5. Cultivate a Mindset of Gratitude:

- **Focus on the positive:** Practice gratitude for the good things in your life, no matter how small they may seem.

- **Appreciate your blessings:** Take time each day to appreciate the gifts and opportunities you have been given.

- **Express gratitude:** Write thank-you notes, tell people you appreciate them, and show your gratitude in meaningful ways.

6. Connect with Others:

- **Find your tribe:** Surround yourself with people who support your dreams and inspire you to grow.

- **Contribute to your community:** Volunteer, mentor others, or participate in activities that make a positive impact.

- **Engage in meaningful conversations:** Engage in conversations that inspire, challenge, and deepen your understanding of the world around you.

7. Embrace a Growth Mindset:

- **View challenges as opportunities:** Embrace challenges as opportunities for learning and growth.
- **Stay curious:** Never stop learning and exploring new ideas and perspectives.
- **Embrace feedback:** Be open to feedback and use it to improve your skills and knowledge.

Living a purpose-driven life is a journey of continual growth and self-discovery. It's about aligning your actions with your values, pursuing your passions, and making a positive impact on the world. Embrace this journey with an open heart and a spirit of adventure, and you will discover a life filled with meaning, joy, and fulfillment.

Remember, it's not about finding the perfect purpose. It's about finding a purpose that resonates with you, that lights you up from within, and that inspires you to live a life that is both meaningful and authentic.

CHAPTER 8

UNLEASHING YOUR CREATIVITY

The Importance of Creativity

Imagine a world where problems become puzzles to solve, and solutions emerge from unexpected corners. That's the power of creativity, a force that unlocks potential, ignites innovation, and redefines the boundaries of what's possible. It's not just about painting masterpieces or composing symphonies; it's about harnessing the power of your imagination to navigate life's complexities and craft a life filled with purpose, joy, and fulfillment.

In this chapter, we embark on a journey to explore the transformative power of creativity. We'll look closely at its profound benefits, explore how it can enhance your well-being, and uncover strategies for unleashing your creative potential.

At its core, creativity is about seeing the world through a new lens, breaking free from conventional thinking, and embracing the unconventional. It's about asking "why?" and "what if?" and venturing beyond the familiar. It's about recognizing that every challenge is an opportunity for innovation, and every obstacle a chance to discover a fresh perspective.

The benefits of cultivating a creative mindset are numerous and far-reaching. It can:

- **Boost your problem-solving skills:** When faced with a challenge, a creative mind doesn't simply seek the most obvious solution. It explores multiple avenues, considers unusual approaches, and often finds unexpected solutions that others might overlook. Think of the inventor who saw the need for a better way to stick notes to walls and transformed communication with the invention of Post-it notes. Creativity wasn't just about inventing a new product; it was about seeing a problem from a different angle.

- **Enhance your communication skills:** Creativity isn't just about ideas; it's about expressing them effectively. A creative mind can find compelling ways to communicate their thoughts, making them more engaging, memorable, and impactful. Whether you're writing a persuasive email, presenting a project, or simply trying to explain a complex concept to a friend, creativity helps you connect with others on a deeper level.

- **Fuel your emotional well-being:** Creativity is a powerful antidote to stress, anxiety, and boredom. Engaging in creative activities allows you to tap into your imagination, express your emotions, and find a sense of peace and joy. Think about the calming effect of coloring, the cathartic release of writing, or the invigorating energy of dancing. These creative outlets can help you manage stress, process emotions, and find a sense of balance in your life.

- **Foster a sense of purpose and meaning:** Creativity can help you discover your passions, tap into your unique talents, and create something meaningful in the world. It allows you to express your individuality, share your gifts with others, and leave your mark on the world. Whether you're a painter, a musician, a writer, or a scientist, creativity allows you to contribute to the world in a unique way.

- **Boost your resilience and adaptability:** The world is constantly changing, and the ability to adapt is essential for thriving in a dynamic environment. A creative mind is adept at finding solutions to unexpected challenges, embracing new opportunities, and navigating change with grace and flexibility. This resilience is a valuable asset in all aspects of life, from personal relationships to professional endeavors.

In a world that often prioritizes logic and efficiency, creativity can feel like a luxury. But it's anything but. It's not a skill reserved for artists and innovators; it's a fundamental human capacity that exists within us all.

It's the spark that ignites the flame of innovation, the wellspring of imagination that fuels a life filled with purpose and meaning. It's the force that allows us to break free from the constraints of the ordinary and embrace the extraordinary.

So, how can you unlock your creative potential? It's not about becoming an artist overnight; it's about cultivating a creative mindset and incorporating creative practices into your daily life. Here are some tips:

- **Embrace curiosity:** Curiosity is the fuel that drives creativity. Ask questions, explore new ideas, and challenge your assumptions. Look for patterns, make connections, and seek out information that expands your knowledge and perspectives.

- **Nurture your imagination:** Allow yourself to dream big. Visualize your ideal future, explore different possibilities, and let your imagination run wild. Don't be afraid to think outside the box and challenge conventional wisdom.

- **Experiment and play:** The most creative breakthroughs often occur when we're not trying too hard. Embrace playful experimentation, try new things, and don't be afraid to make mistakes. Learning from failure is a key ingredient in the creative process.

- **Embrace imperfection:** Don't strive for perfection; embrace the beauty of imperfection. Perfectionism can stifle creativity, so allow yourself to experiment, make mistakes, and learn from them.

- **Cultivate a positive mindset:** A positive outlook can boost your creativity. Focus on the good things in your life, practice gratitude, and surround yourself with positive people. Negative thoughts can stifle creativity, while a positive mindset allows your imagination to flourish.

- **Find your creative outlet:** Explore different forms of creative expression, such as writing, painting, music, dancing, cooking, or gardening. Find something that ignites your passion, allows you to express yourself authentically, and brings you joy.

- **Step outside your comfort zone:** Don't be afraid to try new things, venture into unfamiliar territory, and challenge yourself. The more you stretch your boundaries, the more you'll expand your creative potential.

- **Embrace the power of inspiration:** Inspiration can come from unexpected sources. Pay attention to your surroundings, observe nature, read books, listen to music, and connect with people who inspire you. Allow yourself to be influenced by the world around you and let it spark your creativity.

- **Be persistent:** Creativity is not a magical gift bestowed upon a select few; it's a skill that can be developed with practice and perseverance.

Don't give up if you don't see results immediately. Keep exploring, experimenting, and pushing your boundaries.

In the end, creativity is not about creating masterpieces; it's about embracing the power of your imagination to enhance your life, solve problems, and unlock your full potential. It's about approaching the world with curiosity, embracing the unknown, and finding joy in the journey of discovery.

Embrace the power of your creative mind, and watch as your life transforms into a masterpiece.

Overcoming Creative Blocks

We all have that creative spark within us, waiting to be ignited. It's the force that drives us to imagine, invent, and express ourselves in unique ways. But sometimes, that spark can be dimmed by creative blocks, those annoying mental hurdles that can make it feel like our creativity has gone on vacation, leaving us feeling stuck and uninspired. But fear not! Just like we can train our physical muscles, we can also train our creative muscles to overcome these obstacles and unleash a torrent of fresh ideas.

Imagine a painter facing a blank canvas, a writer staring at a blinking cursor, or a musician struggling to find a melody. It's like a mental fog has descended, obscuring the path to creative expression. These creative blocks can manifest in various forms, each presenting its own unique challenge. Sometimes, they can be as simple as a lack of focus or a case of writer's block, but other times, they can be more complex, rooted in self-doubt, fear of failure, or even the weight of expectations.

One of the most common culprits is **perfectionism**. The desire to create something flawless can paralyze us, preventing us from even starting. We get caught up in the pursuit of the perfect idea, the perfect word, or the perfect note, only to find ourselves paralyzed by the pressure. This can be especially true for beginners, who may feel intimidated by the prospect of creating something that doesn't live up to their own (or others') expectations.

Another roadblock is **fear of failure**. We may be afraid to put our work out there because we're scared of being judged, criticized, or rejected. This fear can keep us trapped in our own heads, preventing us from taking the risks necessary to break through creative barriers. But the truth is, failure is an essential part of the creative process. Every masterpiece is born out of countless failed attempts, discarded ideas, and moments of self-doubt.

Procrastination can also be a significant hurdle. We may put off creative projects, telling ourselves we'll get to them later. But "later" often never comes. The fear of starting, the overwhelming nature of a project, or simply the lure of distractions can all contribute to procrastination. Procrastination, like a thief in the night, steals away valuable time and momentum, hindering our creative progress.

Lack of inspiration can also be a formidable foe. We may feel uninspired, unmotivated, or simply lacking in new ideas. This can be especially common when we're stuck in a rut or feeling overwhelmed by daily life. When inspiration seems to be hiding in the shadows, we may need to actively seek it out, exploring new experiences, stepping outside our comfort zones, and embracing the world with fresh eyes.

But don't despair! Overcoming creative blocks is not about achieving a state of perfect creative flow. It's about understanding the roadblocks, developing strategies to navigate them, and embracing the journey, imperfections and all Here are some powerful strategies to help you conquer those creative hurdles and unleash your full potential:

Embrace the Power of Failure

Failure is not the opposite of success; it's a stepping stone. It's a chance to learn, adapt, and grow. Every time we fail, we gain valuable insights that can help us refine our approach and ultimately achieve greater success. Think of it like a sculptor chipping away at a block of marble, each mistake revealing more of the masterpiece within. The more you embrace failure, the more comfortable you'll become with experimentation, taking risks, and pushing the boundaries of your creativity.

To embrace failure, it's crucial to shift your mindset. Instead of viewing failure as a personal attack or a sign of inadequacy, see it as a valuable opportunity for growth. Ask yourself, "What can I learn from this experience? How can I use this knowledge to improve my next attempt?" Don't be afraid to make mistakes. It's in the process of making and learning from those mistakes that true creativity blossoms.

For instance, imagine a writer who has spent weeks creating the perfect opening line for their novel. They've poured their heart and soul into it, meticulously polishing every word. But when they finally show it to a trusted friend, the feedback is not as positive as they'd hoped. Their friend suggests that the opening line is too predictable and lacks a certain spark. Instead of feeling devastated, the writer embraces this feedback as a valuable learning experience. They realize that their fear of failure had led them to focus too much on perfection and not enough on originality. They decide to experiment with different openings, exploring unexpected voices and perspectives. Through this process of embracing failure, they ultimately discover a more powerful and unique opening that captures the essence of their story.

Embrace the Power of Play

Remember when you were a child, playing with crayons, finger paints, or building elaborate castles out of blocks? Creativity flowed freely, uninhibited by self-doubt or the fear of judgment. We were free to experiment, explore, and express ourselves without holding back. As we grew older, many of us lost touch with that playful spirit, letting the pressures of adulthood dampen our creative spark.

To overcome creative blocks, we can rekindle that playful spirit by embracing the power of play. Allow yourself to experiment, to try new things, to make mistakes, and to enjoy the process without worrying about the outcome. This can mean taking a break from your usual creative routine and trying something completely new. Perhaps you could try a different art medium, explore a new genre of music, or write a poem in a style you've never tried before. The key is to let go of expectations and embrace the joy of creative exploration.

Here are some ways to bring play back into your creative process:

- **Set aside time for free play.** Dedicate a specific time each day or week to engaging in creative activities without any goals or expectations. This could be anything from doodling to writing stream of consciousness to simply letting your imagination run wild.

- **Experiment with different mediums.** If you're a writer, try painting, sculpting, or making music. If you're a musician, try writing poetry or creating visual art. Step outside your comfort zone and see what sparks your imagination.

- **Play with your ideas.** Don't be afraid to experiment with different concepts and approaches. Let your ideas flow freely and don't be afraid to abandon them if they're not working.

- **Don't overthink it.** Creativity thrives on spontaneity and intuition. Don't get bogged down in analysis or try to force ideas. Let your imagination lead the way.

Challenge Your Limiting Beliefs

Our beliefs have a powerful influence on our actions and our creative output. If we believe we're not creative, we're less likely to engage in activities that spark our imagination. These limiting beliefs can be like invisible chains, holding us back from reaching our full potential.

To overcome creative blocks, it's essential to challenge your limiting beliefs. Ask yourself, "Where did these beliefs come from? Are they based on facts or on fear?" Once you've identified your limiting beliefs, you can start to challenge and dismantle them.

Here are some techniques to help you challenge your limiting beliefs:

- **Identify your limiting beliefs.** Pay attention to your thoughts and feelings. What are you telling yourself about your creativity? Are you saying things like, "I'm not creative," "I'm not good enough," or "I'm too old to be creative?"

- **Challenge those beliefs.** Once you've identified your limiting beliefs, start questioning them. Ask yourself, "Is this really true? What evidence do I have to support this belief? What are the benefits of holding onto this belief?"

- **Replace them with empowering beliefs.** Once you've challenged your limiting beliefs, replace them with empowering ones. Start saying things like, "I am creative," "I am capable," and "I have something unique to offer the world."

Remember, your beliefs shape your reality. By challenging your limiting beliefs and replacing them with empowering ones, you can unlock your true creative potential and break through those mental barriers that have been holding you back.

Cultivating a Creative Mindset

Imagine a world where your mind is a fertile garden, bursting with ideas and possibilities. A world where you can tap into a wellspring of creativity, effortlessly generating solutions, creating compelling stories, and expressing yourself in ways that ignite your soul. Cultivating a creative mindset isn't about being born with a natural talent – it's about developing the right conditions for creativity to flourish.

Think of your mind as a canvas. Just as a blank canvas holds the potential for a masterpiece, so too does your mind possess the capacity for boundless creativity. However, like a neglected garden, your mind needs nurturing and attention to blossom with vibrant creativity.

At the heart of a creative mindset lies curiosity. It's the driving force that fuels your exploration of the world, igniting a thirst for knowledge and a fascination with the unknown. Imagine a child's wide-eyed wonder as they discover a new bug, a new book, or a new game. Curiosity allows us to break free from the familiar and embrace the unexpected, challenging our preconceived notions and opening our minds to fresh perspectives.

Open-mindedness, like a welcoming garden gate, allows new ideas and experiences to flow freely. It's the willingness to consider different viewpoints, even those that may initially challenge your own beliefs. Imagine yourself as a traveler exploring a new culture, eager to learn about its customs, traditions, and ways of life. Open-mindedness enables you to appreciate the diversity of human experience, enriching your understanding of the world and inspiring creative expression.

Embrace new experiences as a gardener tending to their plants. Step out of your comfort zone, engage with the world around you, and immerse yourself in new environments, interactions, and perspectives. Whether it's taking a cooking class, attending a concert, or simply having a conversation with someone from a different background, new experiences provide fertile ground for creativity to grow.

Let's explore some practical techniques for cultivating a creative mindset:

- **Embrace the Power of Observation:** Become a mindful observer of your surroundings. Pay attention to the details, the textures, the colors, the sounds, the emotions. Notice the patterns, the rhythms, the unexpected moments that spark your curiosity. Imagine yourself as an artist sketching a scene, capturing the essence of the moment in every stroke.

- **Practice Active Listening:** When you listen to others, truly listen. Engage with their words, their tone, their body language. Ask questions, seek to understand their perspective, and connect with their experiences. Imagine yourself as a storyteller gathering information for a new tale, each conversation a potential source of inspiration.

- **Journaling as a Creative Outlet:** Journaling provides a safe space for your thoughts and ideas to flow freely. It's a sanctuary where you can explore your inner landscape, experiment with different writing styles, and discover hidden gems of creativity. Imagine yourself as a writer creating a story, each entry a chapter in the unfolding narrative of your own creative journey.

- **The Art of Freewriting:** Let your thoughts tumble onto the page without judgment or editing. Don't worry about grammar, punctuation, or structure. Just let your ideas flow, even if they seem random or nonsensical. Imagine yourself as a musician improvising a melody, each note a spontaneous expression of your inner creative energy.

- **Exploring Different Artistic Expressions:** Don't limit yourself to a single form of creative expression. Experiment with different mediums, whether it's painting, sculpting, singing, dancing, or acting. Each art form offers a unique lens through which you can view the world and express yourself. Imagine yourself as a multi-faceted artist, exploring the vast spectrum of human creativity.

- **Embrace Failure as a Stepping Stone:** Failure is not the opposite of success – it's a necessary ingredient. Embrace the lessons learned from missteps and setbacks, viewing them as stepping stones on the path to creative breakthroughs. Imagine yourself as a sculptor shaping a masterpiece, each imperfection a chance to refine and enhance the final product.

- **The Power of Play:** Don't take yourself too seriously. Allow yourself to play, experiment, and explore without fear of judgment. Remember the joy of childhood play – the boundless imagination, the freedom to explore, the acceptance of mistakes as part of the process. Imagine yourself as a child building a castle in the sand, unleashing your creativity without the constraints of adult expectations.

- **Cultivating a Growth Mindset:** Believe in your potential for continuous growth and development. Embrace challenges as opportunities for learning and expanding your creative capabilities. Imagine yourself as a gardener tending to their garden, constantly nurturing and enriching the soil for creativity to flourish.

Cultivating a creative mindset is an ongoing journey, a lifelong adventure in self-discovery and self-expression. It's about embracing the wonder of the world, challenging your own assumptions, and finding joy in the process of creation. So, take a deep breath, open your mind, and let your creativity flourish.

Finding Inspiration in Everyday Life

Inspiration is everywhere, waiting to be discovered. It's like a hidden treasure, concealed in plain sight, waiting for you to open your eyes and your mind to its presence. The key to unlocking inspiration lies in cultivating an attitude of curiosity and openness to the world around you.

Think about a child's sense of wonder. They find amazement in the simplest things – a ladybug crawling on a leaf, the way sunlight dances through the trees, the sound of raindrops hitting the pavement. They haven't yet learned to filter their experiences through the lens of "should" or "shouldn't," allowing them to see the world with fresh, unfiltered eyes.

We can reclaim this childlike curiosity. By actively seeking out inspiration in the mundane, we unlock a wellspring of creative energy. Let's explore some practical ways to cultivate a mindset that welcomes inspiration:

1. The Art of Observation:

Start with simple observations. What do you notice when you walk down the street? Do the colors of the buildings catch your eye? Do you hear the rhythm of footsteps on the sidewalk or the chirping of birds? Pay attention to the patterns in nature – the way leaves grow on a tree, the swirling patterns of a cloud in the sky.

Notice the details, the unexpected, the things that often go unnoticed. This practice of conscious observation sharpens our awareness and opens our minds to new perspectives. It's like a mindful meditation for the senses, allowing us to see the world with fresh eyes.

2. The Power of Experimentation:

Don't be afraid to experiment, to try new things, even if they seem a bit strange or unconventional. Take a different route to work, try a new recipe, listen to a genre of music you've never explored before.

Experimentation is a powerful tool for breaking free from mental ruts and discovering hidden possibilities. It's about embracing uncertainty and stepping outside of your comfort zone, allowing for unexpected discoveries and creative breakthroughs.

3. The Journey of Exploration:

Explore new places, both physically and mentally. Visit a museum, a botanical garden, an art gallery. Read a book on a topic you've never considered before, watch a documentary about a different culture.

Expand your horizons, challenge your preconceived notions, and open yourself up to new ideas and experiences. This kind of exploration expands our perspectives, ignites our imaginations, and fuels our creative fire.

4. The Importance of Routine:

It may seem counterintuitive, but a well-structured routine can actually fuel creativity. When our basic needs are met, when we have a sense of order and structure in our lives, we create a space for inspiration to blossom.

Think of it as tending a garden. We need to provide the right conditions for our creativity to flourish – a consistent watering of discipline and a regular weeding of distractions. This doesn't mean being rigid, but rather establishing a framework that allows us to focus our energy and attention on the things that matter most.

5. The Value of Play:

Remember the joy of play? It's not just for children. Allow yourself to engage in playful activities, to let go of the seriousness and pressure of adult life. Draw, paint, sing, dance, play an instrument, write a story, or just doodle in a notebook.

Play is a powerful antidote to stress and a source of immense joy. It allows us to access our inner child, to let go of inhibitions, and to embrace the freedom of creative expression.

6. The Embrace of Failure:

Failure is an inevitable part of the creative process. It's not something to be feared or avoided, but rather a valuable opportunity for learning and growth. When we embrace failure, we open ourselves up to new possibilities. We learn from our mistakes, refine our approach, and become more resilient in the face of challenges.

Instead of viewing failure as a setback, view it as a stepping stone, a chance to try again, to experiment, to find a new path. Remember, every creative breakthrough is built on a foundation of countless attempts and failures.

7. The Power of Connection:

Surround yourself with people who inspire you. Spend time with friends, family, or colleagues who are passionate about their work, who challenge your perspective, and who make you think differently.

The energy of inspiration is contagious. By surrounding ourselves with people who are creative, passionate, and driven, we amplify our own creative potential.

8. The Importance of Space:

We need space for our creative juices to flow – space to think, space to dream, space to simply be. Make time for solitude, for moments of reflection, for quiet contemplation. Disconnect from the constant noise and demands of the outside world and allow your mind to wander.

This doesn't mean shutting yourself off completely. It means creating intentional space for your inner voice to be heard, for your imagination to soar, for inspiration to strike.

Finding Inspiration in Everyday Life – A Journey of Discovery

Finding inspiration in everyday life is a journey of discovery. It's about opening your eyes, your mind, and your heart to the world around you, to the hidden treasures that lie just beyond the surface.

It's about embracing curiosity, experimentation, exploration, and play. It's about letting go of fear, embracing failure, and connecting with those who inspire you. It's about creating space for your creativity to blossom, for your inner voice to be heard, for your imagination to soar.

Inspiration is all around us. It's in the way sunlight filters through the trees, the sound of laughter echoing through the streets, the warmth of a friendly smile. It's in the unexpected, the unusual, the things that often go unnoticed.

Open your mind, open your heart, and allow yourself to be inspired. The world is full of wonders, waiting to be discovered.

Expressing Your Creativity

Imagine a blank canvas, a fresh sheet of music, or a blank page in a journal. These are the raw materials of creativity, waiting to be filled with the unique expression of your soul. Creativity is not just for artists, musicians, or writers. It's a fundamental part of who we are, a spark that can ignite our lives with joy, purpose, and a sense of fulfillment.

Think about the times you've felt most alive, most connected to your inner self. Perhaps it was when you were lost in a painting, dancing with abandon, composing a song, or writing a story that poured out of you effortlessly. These moments are glimpses of your creative potential, the whispers of your soul longing to be heard.

There's a reason why we feel a sense of satisfaction and peace when we engage in creative pursuits. Creativity is a form of self-expression, a way to connect with our emotions, our thoughts, and our unique perspective on the world. It allows us to process our experiences, make sense of our feelings, and share our inner world with others.

But what if you've never considered yourself creative? What if you feel like your wellspring of inspiration has run dry? Don't be discouraged. Creativity is like a muscle that needs to be exercised and nurtured. It can be cultivated through conscious effort, exploration, and a willingness to embrace the unknown.

Here are some ways to express your creativity:

- **Visual Arts:** Pick up a paintbrush, a pencil, or a camera. Explore different mediums like watercolors, acrylics, charcoal, or digital art. Don't worry about being "good" at it, just let your imagination flow onto the canvas. Create abstract patterns, portraits of loved ones, landscapes that capture your mood, or anything that speaks to your heart.

- **Music:** Experiment with instruments like a guitar, piano, drums, or even your voice. Create melodies, compose songs, or simply play for the joy of making music. Listen to different genres and let them inspire you. Don't be afraid to be unconventional and express yourself in your own unique way.

- **Writing:** Grab a notebook and write down your thoughts, feelings, dreams, or stories. Journaling can be a powerful tool for self-reflection and creative expression. Try writing poetry, short stories, essays, or even just stream-of-consciousness writing. Let the words flow freely without judgment.

- **Dance:** Move your body to the rhythm of music. Explore different dance styles like ballet, modern, jazz, hip-hop, or salsa. Let your body be your instrument and express yourself through movement. Dance like no one is watching and embrace the joy of moving freely.

- **Photography:** Capture moments in time through the lens of a camera. Experiment with different perspectives, angles, and lighting. Find beauty in the ordinary and document the world around you through your unique vision.

- **Cooking:** Transform ingredients into culinary masterpieces. Experiment with flavors, textures, and colors. Create recipes that reflect your personality and inspire others.

- **Gardening:** Cultivate a space of beauty and growth. Plant seeds, nurture plants, and watch them flourish. Experience the satisfaction of creating something from nothing.

- **DIY Projects:** Get your hands dirty and create something tangible. Repair furniture, build a birdhouse, sew a garment, or engage in any project that brings you joy and allows you to express your creativity.

The key is to find outlets that resonate with you, that spark your imagination and bring you a sense of satisfaction. Don't be afraid to try new things, even if you don't think you're "good" at them. The process of creating itself is a form of self-discovery and can lead to unexpected insights and breakthroughs.

Creativity is not about perfection; it's about expression. It's about embracing the freedom to experiment, make mistakes, and learn from the journey. It's about allowing yourself to be vulnerable, to tap into your authentic self, and to share your gifts with the world.

Remember, everyone has creative potential. It's simply a matter of finding your unique voice, your unique style, and your unique way of expressing yourself. So, unleash your creativity, embrace your inner artist, and let your imagination soar. The world is waiting to be inspired by you.

CHAPTER 9

BUILDING A SUCCESSFUL LIFE

Defining Success on Your Own Terms

In the grand tapestry of life, success is often depicted as a shimmering goalpost, a distant horizon that we strive to reach. We're bombarded with societal narratives of what constitutes success the glittering wealth, the prestigious titles, the picture-perfect lifestyle. But what if we told you that success is not a fixed destination, but a journey we create and define for ourselves? What if success is not dictated by external standards, but by the compass of our own hearts and the alignment of our actions with our values?

This is the core of building a successful life, embracing the power to define success on your own terms. It's about breaking free from the mold of what society dictates and creating a blueprint that resonates with your unique spirit, your dreams, and your aspirations. It's about owning your truth and stepping into the authenticity of your being.

Imagine a painter, armed with a palette of vibrant colors, ready to create a masterpiece. The canvas is blank, a blank slate where the painter can express their vision, their emotions, their unique artistic voice. The world might offer a multitude of pre-designed frames, pre-determined themes, or pre-defined expectations. But the true artist, the one who desires to create a masterpiece, will not be bound by these constraints. They will reach into their soul, tap into their innate creativity, and paint a picture that is uniquely their own.

This is the essence of defining success on your own terms. It's about embracing your artistic voice, your unique blend of talents, passions, and dreams. It's about recognizing that the world is not a black and white canvas, but a vibrant spectrum of possibilities, and you have the power to paint your own masterpiece.

Now, let's explore some practical ways to define success on your own terms:

1. Dive Deep into Self-Reflection: The first step towards defining your own success is understanding yourself, your core values, your deepest desires, your aspirations, and your fears. Think of this as a journey of self-discovery, a treasure hunt within your own soul.

- **Journaling:** Dedicate time to journaling, a space where you can express your thoughts, emotions, and aspirations without judgment. Ask yourself questions like: What brings me joy? What truly matters to me? What makes me feel fulfilled?

- **Meditation:** Meditation can be a powerful tool for introspection. Find a quiet space, close your eyes, and observe your thoughts and emotions without judgment. Notice the patterns, the recurring themes, the whispers of your soul.

- **Values Clarification:** Identifying your core values, the guiding principles that shape your life, is crucial. These values can serve as a compass, guiding you towards choices that align with your true self. Consider values such as authenticity, compassion, integrity, creativity, growth, contribution, and freedom.

2. Challenge Conventional Norms: Society often bombards us with predefined notions of success, the big house, the luxury car, the high-paying job. These external markers can create a sense of pressure to conform, to chase an idealized version of success that may not resonate with your true desires.

- **Question Assumptions:** Be willing to question the assumptions that society sets forth. Do you truly believe that success is solely defined by financial wealth or societal status? Are these the things that truly make you feel fulfilled?

- **Define Your Own Measures:** Think beyond the conventional measures of success and identify what truly matters to you. Maybe success for you means having a family, pursuing a creative passion, making a difference in the world, or living a life filled with adventure and purpose.

3. Embrace Your Unique Journey: Every individual's path to success is unique, just like our fingerprints or our DNA. Don't compare your journey to anyone else's. Don't let the highlight reel of others on social media dictate your perception of success.

- **Celebrate Your Uniqueness:** Acknowledge your unique talents, passions, and strengths. Embrace your individuality and create a path that is uniquely your own.

- **Focus on Progress, Not Perfection:** The journey to success is not a linear path. There will be setbacks, detours, and moments of self-doubt. Embrace the process of learning and growing. Focus on the progress you make, not on achieving a perfect outcome.

4. Set Meaningful Goals: Defining your own success is about setting goals that align with your values and aspirations.

- **SMART Goals:** Use the SMART goal framework to create goals that are:
- **Specific:** Clearly define what you want to achieve.
- **Measurable:** Have a way to track your progress.
- **Achievable:** Set goals that are challenging but realistic.
- **Relevant:** Ensure your goals align with your values and aspirations.
- **Time-bound:** Establish a deadline for achieving your goals.
- **Visualize Your Success:** Use visualization techniques to create a mental image of yourself achieving your goals. This can help you stay motivated and focused on your aspirations.

5. Cultivate a Growth Mindset: A growth mindset is the belief that our abilities and intelligence are not fixed, but can be developed through effort and learning. This mindset is crucial for embracing the journey to success, as it allows us to learn from setbacks, adapt to challenges, and continuously grow.

- **Embrace Challenges:** View challenges as opportunities for growth and learning. Don't shy away from stepping outside your comfort zone.
- **Learn from Mistakes:** See mistakes as valuable lessons, not as failures. Use them as opportunities to learn and improve.
- **Believe in Your Ability to Grow:** Trust in your potential to learn and evolve. Have faith in your ability to overcome obstacles and achieve your goals.

6. Prioritize Well-being: Defining success on your own terms is not just about achieving external goals, but also about nurturing your well-being, your physical, mental, and emotional health.

- **Self-Care:** Make self-care a priority. This includes prioritizing your physical health through exercise, proper nutrition, and restful sleep. It also means taking care of your mental and emotional well-being through practices like mindfulness, meditation, and spending time in nature.

- **Surround Yourself with Positivity:** Surround yourself with people who support you, uplift you, and encourage your growth.

- **Celebrate Your Wins:** Acknowledge your progress and celebrate your achievements, big or small. These celebrations can boost your confidence and motivate you to keep moving forward.

Defining success on your own terms is not about attaining a specific destination, but about embarking on a journey of self-discovery, growth, and fulfillment. It's about aligning your actions with your values, embracing your unique path, and creating a life that truly resonates with your spirit. It's about finding joy and meaning in the journey, not just in the destination. And when you define success on your own terms, you unlock the power to create a life that is not only successful, but deeply authentic and fulfilling.

Setting Meaningful Goals

Imagine standing at the precipice of a grand mountain range, its peaks reaching for the heavens. You've traversed a long and winding path, scaling valleys and overcoming challenges to reach this point. Now, as you gaze upon the breathtaking panorama before you, a sense of exhilaration washes over you. You've come so far, and the view is nothing short of awe-inspiring.

This journey, dear reader, is much like your own life. It's a tapestry woven with threads of experiences, both joyous and challenging. Yet, amidst the twists and turns, there lies a profound truth: **your life is a canvas waiting to be painted with the vibrant colors of your dreams.** And to create a masterpiece, you need a clear vision, a guiding force that steers you towards your aspirations.

That guiding force is **the power of goals.**

Goals are the compass that sets your direction, the map that charts your course, and the fuel that ignites your passion. They provide clarity, motivation, and a sense of purpose that propels you forward.

But not all goals are created equal. Some are fleeting desires, while others are deeply rooted aspirations that hold the key to unlocking your true potential. To transform your aspirations into reality, you need to **set meaningful goals.**

And how do you do that? By embracing the **SMART goal-setting framework**, a powerful tool that ensures your goals are clear, actionable, and aligned with your values.

S stands for **Specific**. A specific goal is well-defined, leaving no room for ambiguity. Instead of saying, "I want to be healthier," a specific goal would be, "I want to lose 10 pounds in the next three months."

M represents **Measurable**. A measurable goal allows you to track your progress and celebrate your achievements. Instead of saying, "I want to be more organized," a measurable goal would be, "I want to declutter my home by organizing one room each week."

A is for **Achievable**. An achievable goal is realistic and attainable, challenging you without overwhelming you. Instead of saying, "I want to become a millionaire overnight," an achievable goal would be, "I want to increase my savings by $500 each month."

R signifies **Relevant**. A relevant goal is aligned with your values, interests, and overall life purpose. Instead of saying, "I want to learn to play the piano," a relevant goal would be, "I want to learn to play the piano because it brings me joy and helps me relax."

T stands for **Time-bound**. A time-bound goal has a clear deadline, creating a sense of urgency and accountability. Instead of saying, "I want to write a novel," a time-bound goal would be, "I want to write a novel and complete the first draft by the end of the year."

Think of SMART goals as a **blueprint for your dreams.** They provide structure, clarity, and direction, allowing you to turn your aspirations into tangible achievements.

Consider a young woman named Sarah. She yearned for a career in photography but felt overwhelmed by the vastness of her ambition. One day, she decided to set SMART goals.

- **Her specific goal:** To become a freelance photographer specializing in portraiture.
- **Her measurable goal:** To build a portfolio of 20 high-quality portraits within the next six months.
- **Her achievable goal:** To take a photography workshop and practice shooting portraits at least twice a week.
- **Her relevant goal:** To connect with local businesses and organizations who might need her services.
- **Her time-bound goal:** To secure her first paid photography gig within the next year.

By setting these SMART goals, Sarah created a roadmap for her journey. She felt motivated, focused, and confident in her ability to achieve her dream. Each step she took, each portrait she captured, brought her closer to her ultimate goal.

The power of SMART goals lies in their ability to **transform your dreams into actionable plans.** They break down overwhelming ambitions into manageable steps, allowing you to celebrate each milestone along the way.

Think of setting SMART goals as building a house. You don't just start laying bricks without a blueprint. You need a plan, a vision, and a clear understanding of each step involved.

So, let your dreams be the foundation of your goals, and let the SMART framework be the blueprint for your success.

Here are some additional tips for setting meaningful goals:

- **Connect your goals to your values:** Ask yourself, "What truly matters to me?" Your goals should reflect your deepest beliefs and values.

- **Focus on your strengths:** Identify your talents, skills, and passions. Choose goals that align with your strengths and interests.

- **Visualize your success:** Close your eyes and imagine yourself achieving your goals. The more vivid your visualization, the more powerful it becomes.

- **Seek feedback and support:** Share your goals with trusted friends, family, or mentors. Their feedback can help you refine your plans and stay motivated.

- **Break down large goals into smaller steps:** Overwhelming goals can feel daunting. Break them down into smaller, achievable tasks.

- **Celebrate your milestones:** Acknowledge and celebrate your accomplishments along the way. This helps to maintain your motivation and reinforce your commitment.

Remember, setting meaningful goals isn't just about achieving your dreams; it's about **creating a life that is authentic, purposeful, and fulfilling.**

It's about **embracing the journey, learning from your experiences, and becoming the best version of yourself.**

Now that you've set your sights on the horizon, it's time to **take the first step.**

The path ahead may have its challenges, but with a clear vision, a commitment to action, and the power of SMART goal-setting, you're ready to conquer any mountain. The view from the top will be worth every step of the way.

Overcoming Procrastination

Procrastination is a thief of time and a saboteur of dreams. We all succumb to its insidious grip from time to time, putting off tasks, big and small, until the last possible moment. This procrastination often stems from a myriad of factors, from fear of failure to a lack of clarity and motivation.

But the good news is that procrastination is not an insurmountable obstacle. It's a habit, and like any habit, it can be broken. The journey to overcoming procrastination begins with understanding its roots and then equipping ourselves with the tools and strategies to tackle it head-on.

The Roots of Procrastination:

- **Fear of Failure:** Procrastination can be a defense mechanism to avoid the potential disappointment of not meeting our own expectations. The fear of failing can paralyze us, making us hesitant to even start a task.

- **Perfectionism:** The desire to produce flawless work can lead to procrastination. We might spend an inordinate amount of time planning and revising, fearing that anything less than perfect won't suffice.

- **Lack of Clarity:** When we lack a clear understanding of what needs to be done, it can feel overwhelming. We may avoid starting a task because we don't know where to begin or how to approach it effectively.

- **Lack of Motivation:** Sometimes, procrastination simply arises from a lack of interest or enthusiasm for the task at hand. It's easy to put off something that doesn't excite us or feel particularly important.

- **Overwhelm:** Facing a large, complex task can feel daunting. The sheer volume of the project can make us want to avoid it altogether, hoping it will magically disappear or become less demanding.

- **Distractions:** In today's technology-driven world, we are constantly bombarded with distractions. Social media, emails, and notifications can easily derail our focus, leading us to procrastinate on tasks that require our undivided attention.

Strategies for Overcoming Procrastination:

- **Break It Down:** The most effective way to tackle a daunting task is to break it down into smaller, manageable steps. Divide the project into smaller chunks, and focus on completing one step at a time. This approach helps alleviate overwhelm and makes the task feel less daunting.

- **Set Realistic Goals:** Set realistic goals and expectations for yourself. Aim for progress, not perfection. Don't expect to accomplish everything overnight. Start with small steps and gradually build momentum.

- **Prioritize and Schedule:** Identify the most important tasks and prioritize them accordingly. Create a schedule that allocates time for each task and stick to it as much as possible.

- **Eliminate Distractions:** Create a distraction-free environment to focus on your work. Turn off your phone, close unnecessary tabs, and find a quiet space where you can concentrate without interruptions.

- **Start Small:** Sometimes, the hardest part is getting started. Even a small step can create momentum. Begin with a small portion of the task, even if it's just five minutes of work. This can help overcome inertia and create a sense of accomplishment.

- **Time Blocking:** Allocate specific blocks of time for each task and stick to them. This helps maintain focus and prevent time from slipping away unnecessarily.

- **Reward Yourself:** Reward yourself for making progress. Acknowledge your efforts and celebrate small wins along the way. This helps maintain motivation and reinforces positive behavior.

- **Seek Support:** Don't be afraid to ask for support from friends, family, or colleagues. Sharing your goals and challenges can create accountability and encourage you to stay on track.

- **Practice Mindfulness:** Mindfulness can help you become more aware of your thoughts and feelings. It can help you identify the triggers that lead to procrastination and develop strategies for managing them.

- **Challenge Negative Thoughts:** Negative thoughts can sabotage your efforts. Challenge any negative self-talk that arises and replace it with positive affirmations. Remind yourself of your strengths and abilities.

- **Embrace Failure:** Failure is a natural part of the learning process. Don't let it discourage you. View setbacks as opportunities to learn and grow.

- **Cultivate a Growth Mindset:** Embrace a growth mindset, believing that your abilities can be developed through hard work and dedication. Focus on continuous improvement and learning rather than simply striving for perfection.

The Power of Action:

Overcoming procrastination is not a magical overnight fix. It's a journey that requires conscious effort and commitment. The key is to take action, no matter how small. Start with one step, then another, and build momentum until you reach your goals.

Remember, procrastination is not a sign of weakness. It's a common human experience that can be overcome with self-awareness, perseverance, and a willingness to embrace change.

Developing Strong Work Habits

Imagine a world where you wake up each morning feeling energized and focused, ready to tackle your to-do list with a sense of purpose. This isn't just a dream; it's a reality that can be achieved by developing strong work habits. Think of these habits as your secret weapons, empowering you to conquer your goals and build a life that is both productive and fulfilling.

The foundation of strong work habits lies in establishing a consistent routine. Just as a well-oiled machine runs smoothly, a structured schedule can streamline your days and eliminate wasted time. Start by identifying your peak productivity hours. Some people thrive in the early morning hours, while others find their creative flow in the late evenings. Once you know your optimal working times, carve out dedicated blocks in your schedule for focused work. This will create a sense of rhythm and predictability, making it easier to stay on track.

Time management is another crucial element of successful work habits. In today's fast-paced world, it's easy to feel overwhelmed by the sheer volume of tasks on our plates. The key is to prioritize. This means identifying the most important tasks that will move you closer to your goals and tackling them first. One helpful strategy is to employ the Eisenhower Matrix, a tool that categorizes tasks based on urgency and importance. Focus your energy on tasks that are both urgent and important, delegate or postpone those that are less critical, and eliminate tasks that hold no value.

Staying organized is essential for maintaining productive work habits. A cluttered desk can easily lead to a cluttered mind, making it difficult to concentrate and stay motivated. Invest in a system that works for you, whether it's a physical planner, a digital calendar, or a combination of both. Regularly review your to-do list and prioritize tasks based on their deadlines and importance. Don't be afraid to break down large tasks into smaller, more manageable steps. This will make them feel less daunting and make progress easier to track.

Beyond organization, developing a positive work environment is crucial for maintaining focus and motivation. Surround yourself with inspiration, whether it's motivational quotes, inspiring images, or a view of nature. Create a space that is comfortable, well-lit, and free from distractions. Consider investing in noise-canceling headphones or finding a quiet corner of your home or office to work.

Building strong work habits requires discipline and commitment. There will be days when it's tempting to slack off or succumb to distractions. But just like any muscle, your work habits need to be exercised regularly. Start small and gradually increase your focus and productivity. Reward yourself for making progress and celebrate your successes, no matter how small.

The journey to developing strong work habits is not a destination, but a continuous process. It's about constantly refining your routines, experimenting with different strategies, and adapting your approach to fit your changing needs. Remember that the key to success is consistency and dedication.

Here are some additional tips for developing strong work habits:

- **Start your day with a clear intention:** Begin each day with a purpose. What are your top priorities for the day? Visualize yourself successfully completing these tasks and set the tone for a productive day.

- **Batch similar tasks:** Instead of constantly switching between different tasks, group similar tasks together. This can help you achieve a state of flow and get more done in less time.

- **Eliminate distractions:** Identify the biggest distractions in your work environment and find ways to eliminate them. This might mean turning off social media notifications, closing unnecessary browser tabs, or finding a quiet place to work.

- **Take regular breaks:** Our brains can only focus for a limited period. Taking regular breaks can help you refresh your mind and return to your work with renewed energy.

- **Celebrate your progress:** Don't underestimate the power of positive reinforcement. Celebrate your accomplishments, big or small, and reward yourself for making progress. This will help you stay motivated and committed to your goals.

Remember, developing strong work habits is an investment in your future. It empowers you to achieve your goals, improve your productivity, and live a life that is both fulfilling and successful. So, take a deep breath, embrace the power of routine, and embark on your journey to building a life you love.

Embracing Continuous Learning

Imagine a vast library, its shelves overflowing with knowledge, wisdom, and countless stories waiting to be discovered. Each book represents a potential adventure, a new skill to learn, or a perspective to expand. This library is not a physical space, but rather a boundless realm of information available to us all, thanks to the wonders of the internet and the relentless pursuit of human curiosity.

In this ever evolving world, where information is constantly being updated and new discoveries are made daily, remaining stagnant is akin to letting a beautiful garden wither and fade. It's an invitation to embrace the spirit of lifelong learning, a journey that never truly ends.

Consider the life of a seasoned chef, who, after years of perfecting their craft, still dedicates time to attending cooking classes, experimenting with new techniques, and exploring the cuisines of different cultures. They know that true mastery comes from a constant thirst for knowledge and a willingness to push boundaries.

The same principle applies to every aspect of our lives, from personal relationships to career pursuits. Learning doesn't have to be confined to formal education or structured courses. It can be as simple as reading a book outside your comfort zone, attending a workshop, engaging in meaningful conversations with people from different backgrounds, or even taking an online course on a topic that piques your interest.

The act of learning doesn't always need to be driven by practical goals or career aspirations. It can be fueled by pure curiosity, a desire to explore new ideas, and a thirst to understand the world around us better. Consider the joy of immersing yourself in a fascinating documentary, uncovering hidden stories in historical archives, or simply allowing yourself to be captivated by a captivating podcast. These experiences, while seemingly trivial, can expand our horizons, challenge our assumptions, and spark new passions.

Think back to the times in your life when you felt truly alive and engaged. Chances are, those moments were fueled by a sense of discovery, a thirst for knowledge, and a willingness to step outside your comfort zone. It might have been the exhilarating feeling of mastering a new skill, the sense of accomplishment that came from understanding a complex concept, or the profound connection you felt after engaging in a thought-provoking conversation.

So, how can we cultivate this lifelong thirst for learning and make it an integral part of our lives? Here are a few practical tips to get you started:

- **Embrace the Power of Curiosity:** Ask questions, explore new topics, and never be afraid to admit that you don't know something.

- **Make Learning a Habit:** Set aside dedicated time for learning, even if it's just 15 minutes a day. Read a book, listen to a podcast, watch a documentary, or take an online course.

- **Seek out Mentors and Role Models:** Surround yourself with people who inspire you and can guide you on your journey.

- **Experiment and Try New Things:** Step outside your comfort zone and explore new activities, hobbies, or skills.

- **Embrace Failure as a Learning Opportunity:** Don't be afraid to make mistakes. View them as stepping stones on your path to growth and mastery.

Remember, the journey of learning is a lifelong adventure, full of unexpected twists and turns. It's not about achieving a specific destination but rather about embracing the process of continuous growth, discovery, and expansion. So, let your curiosity lead the way, keep an open mind, and never stop learning. The world is your classroom, and the possibilities are endless.

CHAPTER 10

MASTERING YOUR FINANCES

Understanding Your Financial Situation

The first step in gaining control over your finances is understanding where your money is going. It's like trying to navigate a maze without a map - you might stumble around, but you're unlikely to reach your destination.

Imagine you're trying to lose weight. You wouldn't just blindly start running without first understanding how many calories you consume daily. You'd need to track your intake to see where you can make changes. The same applies to your finances. You need to understand your financial situation before you can begin to improve it.

Taking Stock of Your Current Finances

Start by honestly assessing your current financial situation. Gather all your financial documents, including bank statements, credit card bills, loan statements, and investment statements. This information will give you a clear picture of your income, expenses, assets, and debts.

Budgeting: The Foundation of Financial Control

A budget is a plan for how you'll spend your money. It's your roadmap to financial stability. By creating a budget, you can:

- **Track Your Spending:** You'll become more aware of where your money is going.
- **Identify Areas for Savings:** You can uncover areas where you can cut back on unnecessary spending.
- **Plan for Your Future:** You can allocate funds towards your financial goals, like saving for retirement or paying off debt.

There are many ways to create a budget. You can use a spreadsheet, a budgeting app, or even a simple notebook. The key is to find a method that works best for you.

Tracking Expenses: Unveiling the Hidden Costs

You can't control what you don't track. Tracking your expenses is essential for understanding where your money is going and identifying areas for savings. You can use a budgeting app, a spreadsheet, or even a simple notepad to track your expenses.

Understanding Debt: The Burden You Can Overcome

Debt can feel like an overwhelming burden. But by understanding it, you can develop a plan to manage it effectively.

Start by identifying all your debts, including credit cards, student loans, mortgages, and personal loans. For each debt, note:

- **The Principal Amount:** The original amount you borrowed.

- **The Interest Rate:** The percentage charged on the borrowed amount.
- **The Minimum Payment:** The amount you need to pay each month to avoid late fees.

Developing a Plan to Manage Your Debt

Once you understand your debt, you can develop a plan to manage it effectively. Here are some common strategies:

- **Debt Consolidation:** Combining multiple debts into a single loan with a lower interest rate can save you money on interest payments.
- **Debt Snowball Method:** Paying off the smallest debt first, even if it has a higher interest rate, can give you a sense of accomplishment and motivate you to continue paying down your debts.
- **Debt Avalanche Method:** Paying off the debt with the highest interest rate first can save you the most money in the long run.

Creating a Financial Strategy: Your Blueprint for Success

Developing a financial strategy is like creating a blueprint for your financial future. It involves setting financial goals, creating a budget, and managing your debt. Here's a step-by-step guide:

- **Define Your Financial Goals:** What do you want to achieve financially? Do you want to save for retirement, buy a house, or pay off your debts?
- **Create a Realistic Budget:** Based on your income and expenses, create a budget that you can stick to.
- **Track Your Progress:** Regularly review your budget and track your progress toward your financial goals.

- **Stay Disciplined:** Stick to your budget and make adjustments as needed.
- **Seek Professional Advice:** If you feel overwhelmed, consider seeking advice from a financial advisor.

Taking Charge of Your Finances

Mastering your finances is a journey, not a destination. It requires effort, discipline, and a willingness to learn. But by understanding your financial situation, creating a budget, and developing a plan to manage your debt, you can gain control over your financial future.

Remember, it's never too late to start. The sooner you begin, the sooner you can start living a more financially secure and fulfilling life.

Setting Financial Goals

Financial goals are the cornerstones of a secure and fulfilling future. They provide direction, motivation, and a sense of purpose to your financial journey. Setting financial goals is not about depriving yourself; it's about taking control of your financial destiny and paving the way for a brighter tomorrow.

Imagine a future where you're financially free, able to pursue your passions without the constant worry of money. That's the power of setting and achieving financial goals. But where do you begin? The journey starts with understanding your current financial standing, your aspirations, and the steps you need to take to bridge the gap between where you are and where you want to be.

Step 1: Assess Your Current Financial Landscape

Before embarking on a goal-setting expedition, you need a map. This map is your current financial picture, a snapshot of your income, expenses, assets, and debts. This self-assessment is crucial for gaining clarity and identifying areas for improvement.

- **Income:** List all sources of income, including your salary, investments, rental income, or any other regular inflow of funds.

- **Expenses:** Analyze your spending patterns. Create a detailed list of all your monthly expenses, from groceries and rent to entertainment and subscriptions. This step might be eye-opening, revealing areas where you could cut back.

- **Assets:** Assets are what you own, such as your house, car, savings, investments, and any valuable possessions.

- **Debts:** List all your debts, including mortgages, loans, credit card balances, and any outstanding bills.

Step 2: Define Your Financial Goals

With a clear understanding of your current financial situation, you can now start to define your financial goals. These goals should be specific, measurable, achievable, relevant, and time-bound (SMART).

- **Saving for Retirement:** Retirement might seem distant, but starting early is key. Determine how much you want to save for a comfortable retirement and set a realistic timeline for reaching your goal.

- **Buying a Home:** Owning a home is often a significant financial goal. Determine the type of home you desire, calculate the estimated cost, and research mortgage options.

- **Paying Off Debt:** Debt can be a significant financial burden. Prioritize paying off high-interest debts, such as credit cards, to reduce your overall interest burden.

- **Saving for Emergencies:** Life throws curveballs. Building an emergency fund can provide a safety net for unexpected expenses or job losses. Aim for 3 to 6 months' worth of living expenses.

- **Investing for the Future:** Investing is essential for building wealth over time. Determine your investment goals and risk tolerance, and research different investment options, such as stocks, bonds, mutual funds, or real estate.

- **Reaching a Specific Financial Milestone:** Perhaps you want to save for a down payment on a car, fund a child's education, or take a dream vacation. Set a clear goal, determine the amount you need to save, and create a plan to achieve it.

Step 3: Create a Budget and Track Your Expenses

A budget is your roadmap to achieving your financial goals. It provides a clear picture of where your money goes and helps you identify areas where you can cut back or reallocate funds.

- **Track Your Spending:** Keep a detailed record of your expenses for a month or two to identify areas where you can save. Use a budgeting app, spreadsheet, or even a notebook to keep track.

- **Prioritize Needs vs. Wants:** Differentiate between essential needs (housing, food, transportation) and wants (entertainment, dining out, shopping).

- **Allocate Funds:** Once you know where your money is going, you can allocate funds to your financial goals. This could involve setting aside a certain amount each month for savings, debt repayment, or investing.

- **Review and Adjust:** Regularly review your budget and adjust it as needed based on changes in your income or expenses.

Step 4: Implement Strategies for Financial Success

Achieving your financial goals requires discipline and consistent action. Here are some effective strategies to help you stay on track:

- **Automate Your Savings:** Set up automatic transfers from your checking account to your savings account each month. This takes the effort out of saving and ensures that you consistently contribute to your goals.

- **Negotiate Your Bills:** Contact your service providers (internet, phone, cable) and see if you can negotiate lower rates. You might be surprised at how much you can save by simply asking.

- **Reduce Unnecessary Expenses:** Examine your spending patterns and identify areas where you can cut back. This could involve reducing subscriptions, limiting dining out, or finding alternative ways to entertain yourself.

- **Increase Your Income:** Consider ways to increase your income, such as taking on a side hustle, asking for a raise, or negotiating a better salary in a new job.

- **Seek Financial Advice:** If you're struggling to manage your finances or need guidance on investing or planning for retirement, consider seeking advice from a financial advisor. They can provide personalized recommendations and help you develop a tailored financial plan.

Step 5: Stay Motivated and Celebrate Success

Reaching your financial goals is a marathon, not a sprint. It requires dedication, perseverance, and a positive mindset.

- **Visualize Your Goals:** Take time each day to visualize yourself achieving your financial goals. This will help you stay motivated and focused on your journey.

- **Reward Yourself:** As you achieve milestones along the way, reward yourself with something small but meaningful. This will help you stay engaged and motivated.

- **Stay Informed:** Keep up-to-date on financial news and trends to make informed decisions about your money.

- **Seek Support:** Share your financial goals with friends, family, or a financial advisor for encouragement and accountability.

Remember, financial success is not a destination, but a journey. Each small step you take towards your financial goals, no matter how seemingly insignificant, contributes to your overall financial well-being and builds a brighter future for yourself.

Creating a Budget and Managing Expenses

Creating a budget and managing expenses effectively are fundamental skills for achieving financial freedom. It's like building a sturdy foundation for your financial house; without a solid budget, your money can easily slip through the cracks.

Imagine your budget as a roadmap, guiding you towards your financial goals. Just like a well-planned journey, you need to know where you're going and how you'll get there. To craft a realistic budget, we need to understand where your money is going. Start by tracking your income and expenses for a month or two. This might seem tedious, but it's like taking an inventory of your financial resources.

Once you have a clear picture of your income and expenses, you can begin creating your budget. There are various budgeting methods available, but the key is to find one that works for you. Some popular methods include the 50/30/20 rule, the zero-based budget, and the envelope system.

The 50/30/20 rule suggests allocating 50% of your income towards needs (such as rent, groceries, utilities), 30% towards wants (such as entertainment, dining out), and 20% towards savings and debt repayment. The zero-based budget involves allocating every dollar of your income to a specific category, leaving no room for unplanned spending. The envelope system involves placing cash into physical envelopes for different categories, such as groceries, gas, and entertainment.

When creating your budget, remember that prioritizing needs over wants is crucial. This might mean cutting back on some luxuries to ensure that you have enough money for essential expenses like housing, food, and transportation. It's like deciding to prioritize your health over indulging in unhealthy snacks.

Beyond creating a budget, managing expenses effectively is vital. Here are some practical tips:

- **Set realistic financial goals:** Think about your short-term and long-term financial goals. Perhaps you want to save for a vacation or pay off a loan. Setting clear goals will help you stay motivated and track your progress.

- **Track your spending:** Use a budgeting app or a spreadsheet to monitor your spending habits. This will help you identify areas where you can cut back or save more. It's like having a personal financial assistant who helps you stay accountable.

- **Look for opportunities to save:** Explore ways to save money on everyday expenses. For example, cook at home more often, use coupons, or negotiate better deals.

- **Avoid impulse purchases:** Resist the urge to buy things you don't need. Think about whether the purchase is truly necessary or just a temporary whim.

- **Create a "no-spend" day or week:** Challenge yourself to spend zero dollars for a day or a week. This can help you break bad spending habits and gain a greater appreciation for your financial resources.

- **Automate your savings:** Set up automatic transfers from your checking account to your savings account. This way, you won't have to think about it, and you'll be saving money consistently. It's like having a financial robot that does your saving for you.

- **Cut unnecessary subscriptions:** Review your subscriptions and cancel any services you're not using. It's like decluttering your financial life and getting rid of unwanted expenses.

- **Negotiate your bills:** Don't be afraid to call your cable company, phone company, or insurance company to see if you can get a better rate.

- **Consider side hustles:** Think about starting a side hustle to earn extra income. This can help you reach your financial goals faster and give you more financial flexibility.

Remember, financial freedom is not about being wealthy; it's about having the control and confidence to make informed financial decisions that align with your values and goals. Just like a skilled navigator, you can chart your financial course with careful planning, consistent effort, and a bit of financial discipline.

Building a Strong Financial Foundation

Building a strong financial foundation is like building a sturdy house. It takes time, effort, and a solid plan. Just as a well-constructed house can withstand storms and provide a secure haven, a robust financial foundation can weather life's unexpected twists and turns and offer peace of mind.

Investing: Seeding Your Financial Future

Imagine a seed, small and seemingly insignificant, planted in fertile ground. With time, care, and nourishment, it grows into a magnificent tree, providing shade, sustenance, and beauty. Investing is akin to planting those financial seeds, allowing your money to grow and multiply over time.

There are many different ways to invest, from buying stocks and bonds to investing in real estate or precious metals. The key is to understand your risk tolerance, your financial goals, and the time horizon for your investments. Just as you wouldn't plant a sunflower seed in the desert, you wouldn't invest in a high-risk asset if you need the money in the short term.

Saving: Building a Financial Buffer

Saving is like building a financial safety net, providing a cushion for unexpected expenses or financial emergencies. It's a habit that requires discipline and consistency, but the rewards are well worth the effort. Think of it as putting aside a portion of your income for a rainy day, ensuring you have a financial lifeline when you need it most.

The key to effective saving is to automate it. Setting up regular transfers from your checking account to your savings account can help you build a healthy nest egg without even thinking about it. Start small, even if it's just a few dollars a week, and gradually increase the amount as your income grows.

Minimizing Debt: Breaking the Cycle of Interest

Debt can feel like a heavy weight, dragging you down and preventing you from reaching your financial goals. It's a cycle that can be difficult to break, but with a strategic approach, you can regain control of your finances.

The first step is to understand the nature of your debt. Differentiate between good debt, such as a mortgage or a student loan, and bad debt, like credit card debt or payday loans. Good debt can help you build wealth or acquire assets, while bad debt often comes with high interest rates and can lead to financial instability.

Once you understand your debt situation, create a plan to pay it down. Prioritize high-interest debt, such as credit cards, and focus on making more than the minimum payment whenever possible. Consider a debt consolidation loan or a balance transfer to lower your interest rate and make it easier to repay.

Strategies for Success

Building a strong financial foundation is a journey, not a destination. It requires a blend of patience, perseverance, and informed decision-making. Here are some strategies to help you navigate your financial path:

- **Budgeting:** A budget is like a roadmap, guiding you towards your financial goals. It helps you track your income, expenses, and savings, ensuring you stay on track and avoid overspending.

- **Financial Literacy:** The more you understand about finance, the better equipped you are to make sound decisions. Take the time to learn about investing, saving, debt management, and other financial concepts.

- **Seek Professional Advice:** Don't be afraid to ask for help. A financial advisor can provide personalized guidance and help you develop a comprehensive financial plan.

- **Be Patient and Consistent:** Building wealth takes time. Stay consistent with your savings and investment plan, and don't get discouraged by short-term fluctuations in the market.

A Life of Financial Freedom

Imagine a life free from financial worry, where you can pursue your passions, travel the world, or simply enjoy the peace of mind that comes with financial security. Building a strong financial foundation is the first step towards achieving this dream.

By investing in your future, saving diligently, and minimizing debt, you can create a solid financial foundation that empowers you to live a life of purpose, fulfillment, and financial freedom. Remember, your financial journey is unique, and it's up to you to chart your course and navigate towards your desired destination.

Achieving Financial Freedom

Imagine a life where you're not constantly worrying about money, where you have the freedom to pursue your passions, and where financial security is no longer a distant dream. This is the essence of financial freedom. It is a state of mind where you're in control of your finances, not the other way around. It's not just about having a lot of money; it's about having the knowledge and skills to manage your money wisely, allowing you to live life on your terms.

Financial literacy is the key to unlocking this freedom. It's about understanding how money works, from budgeting and saving to investing and debt management. Think of it as a superpower that empowers you to make informed financial decisions and take control of your financial future.

But why is financial literacy so important? It's more than just managing your bills; it's about securing your future, achieving your dreams, and living a life free from financial stress.

Let's break down the reasons why financial literacy is so crucial:

1. Reducing Financial Stress:

Have you ever felt overwhelmed by bills, debt, or the constant worry about money? Financial literacy can help you understand your spending habits, create a budget, and develop strategies to manage your money effectively. This can significantly reduce financial stress, allowing you to focus on other aspects of your life. Imagine waking up each morning without the burden of financial worries weighing you down.

2. Achieving Financial Goals:

Whether it's buying a home, starting a business, retiring comfortably, or traveling the world, financial literacy empowers you to set realistic financial goals and create a plan to achieve them. By understanding the principles of saving, investing, and budgeting, you can turn your dreams into reality.

3. Building a Secure Future:

Financial literacy provides a safety net for unforeseen circumstances. Imagine facing a job loss, a medical emergency, or a natural disaster. Having a financial cushion built through smart savings and investments can help you weather these storms and maintain stability.

4. Making Informed Financial Decisions:

Financial literacy empowers you to make informed decisions about everything from borrowing money to investing. It helps you understand the risks and rewards associated with various financial products and services, allowing you to choose the options that align with your goals and financial well-being.

5. Breaking Free from Debt Cycles:

Debt can be a significant burden, limiting your financial flexibility and preventing you from reaching your goals. By understanding the different types of debt, interest rates, and repayment strategies, financial literacy empowers you to break free from debt cycles and build a healthier financial future.

6. Investing for a Brighter Future:

Investing is a key component of financial freedom. Financial literacy equips you with the knowledge to understand different investment options, assess risk, and make smart investment decisions. This can help you grow your wealth over time and achieve your long-term financial goals.

7. Passing Down Financial Wisdom to Future Generations:

By becoming financially literate, you can not only improve your own financial well-being but also pass on valuable knowledge to your children or loved ones. This can help them develop healthy financial habits from a young age and build a secure financial future.

Financial literacy is not just about numbers and spreadsheets; it's about taking control of your life and shaping your future. It's about empowering yourself to make choices that align with your values and aspirations, allowing you to live a life free from financial constraints.

Here's how you can embark on your journey to financial freedom:

1. Start with Self-Awareness:

The first step is to take a clear look at your current financial situation. Track your income and expenses for a few months to get a realistic picture of your spending habits. Identify areas where you can cut back or make adjustments.

2. Set SMART Financial Goals:

Once you have a clear understanding of your current finances, set realistic financial goals that are specific, measurable, achievable, relevant, and time-bound. This could include saving for a down payment on a house, paying off debt, or building a retirement nest egg.

3. Create a Budget:

A budget is a roadmap to your financial goals. Create a budget that allocates your income to different categories such as housing, food, transportation, and entertainment. Stick to your budget as closely as possible to stay on track with your financial goals.

4. Build a Savings Plan:

Saving is crucial for financial security and achieving your goals. Start by setting a savings goal and automating your savings by transferring a set amount from your checking account to your savings account each month.

5. Explore Investment Options:

Investing can help your money grow over time and achieve your long-term financial goals. Start by researching different investment options, considering your risk tolerance and financial goals. You can consult with a financial advisor to get personalized guidance.

6. Manage Debt Wisely:

Debt can be a significant obstacle to achieving financial freedom. Prioritize paying off high-interest debt first, and explore options like debt consolidation to simplify your repayment process.

7. Continue Learning:

Financial literacy is an ongoing process. Keep up with financial news and trends, read books and articles on personal finance, and attend workshops or seminars to expand your knowledge.

Financial freedom is not a destination; it's a journey. Embrace the opportunity to learn, grow, and take control of your financial future. The power to create a life of financial abundance lies within you, waiting to be unleashed.

CHAPTER 11

EMBRACING CHANGE AND GROWTH

The Inevitability of Change

Change is a constant companion, a dance partner in the waltz of life. It whispers in the rustling leaves, roars in the crashing waves, and hums in the rhythm of our beating hearts. Some changes are gentle, like the sun warming the earth in spring, while others are sudden and forceful, like a storm that sweeps across the land. Each change carries within it the potential for growth, transformation, and an evolution of the soul.

From the moment we are born, we are caught in the current of change. We learn to crawl, then walk, then run, each milestone a testament to the relentless power of transformation. Our bodies grow and shift, our minds expand, and our perspectives evolve. The world around us is also in a state of constant flux, technology races forward, society redefines its norms, and even the earth itself undergoes constant geological change.

Yet, amidst this relentless cycle, there is a sense of comfort. Change, like the seasons, is a natural phenomenon, a predictable rhythm that underpins our existence. Embracing this inherent truth allows us to navigate the choppy waters of life with a sense of calm. We understand that change is not a force to be feared but an opportunity to be embraced.

Imagine a caterpillar cocooned in a chrysalis. It seems to be static, perhaps even stagnant, but beneath the surface, a magnificent metamorphosis is unfolding. The caterpillar's cells are dividing and rearranging, reimagining themselves into something new and extraordinary. Finally, the chrysalis cracks open, and a butterfly emerges, its wings delicate and iridescent, ready to dance among the flowers. This is the essence of change: a beautiful and essential transformation that takes us from one state of being to another, often leading us to a higher level of consciousness and understanding.

However, the path of change is not always smooth. Resistance often arises, a natural response to the unknown. We cling to the familiar, fear stepping outside our comfort zones, and yearn for the safety of the status quo. Yet, it is in these moments of resistance that we have the opportunity to grow the most. For it is in the face of challenge that our true strength and resilience are revealed.

Imagine a climber scaling a mountain. The path is treacherous, the air thin, and the temptation to turn back is strong. But the climber perseveres, pushing past their fears, their muscles burning, their breath ragged. With each arduous step, they build strength, develop stamina, and gain a newfound appreciation for their capabilities. In the end, when they reach the summit, they are not the same person who set out on the journey. They are transformed, stronger, wiser, and more confident.

Change is a powerful force that can propel us forward, but we must learn to harness its energy. We must cultivate a sense of curiosity, a willingness to explore the unknown, and an openness to new possibilities. We must remember that change is not the enemy, but a necessary catalyst for growth and transformation.

There are many ways to embrace change and unlock its potential. Here are a few strategies to consider:

- **Embrace a Growth Mindset:** Instead of viewing challenges as setbacks, view them as opportunities for growth and learning. Cultivate a belief in your ability to learn, adapt, and evolve. A growth mindset allows you to embrace change with a sense of curiosity and a willingness to learn from your experiences.

- **Practice Mindfulness:** Mindfulness is the practice of paying attention to the present moment without judgment. It allows you to observe your thoughts, feelings, and sensations without getting carried away by them. By being present in the moment, you can respond to change with greater awareness and clarity. Meditation, yoga, and deep breathing exercises can help develop mindfulness.

- **Set Clear Goals and Intentions:** When faced with change, it is helpful to have a sense of direction. Setting goals and intentions allows you to navigate change with purpose and focus. It provides a sense of clarity and helps you to stay aligned with your values and aspirations.

- **Visualize Your Desired Outcome:** Visualizing your desired outcome is a powerful tool for manifesting change. By creating a clear picture in your mind of what you want to achieve, you activate the power of your subconscious mind and increase the likelihood of success.

- **Celebrate Your Progress:** Acknowledge and celebrate your progress along the way. Recognize the small victories, big or small, and acknowledge the effort you have made. This helps to maintain motivation and reinforces your belief in your ability to change.

- **Surround Yourself with Positive Influences:** Surround yourself with people who inspire you, support you, and believe in your potential.

Their energy and positivity can help you to navigate change with confidence and resilience.

- **Embrace Imperfection:** Change is a process, not a destination. It is a journey of growth and evolution, and it is natural to experience setbacks and challenges along the way. Embrace imperfection, learn from your mistakes, and continue to move forward.

Change is a constant companion, an essential ingredient in the recipe of life. It is a force that can reshape us, refine us, and ultimately, help us to become the best versions of ourselves. By embracing change with curiosity, courage, and a growth mindset, we unlock its transformative power and embark on a journey of continuous growth and fulfillment.

Adapting to Change and Uncertainty

Life throws curveballs. It's a constant dance of change and uncertainty, a rollercoaster ride that can leave us feeling dizzy and disoriented. But amidst the turbulence, lies an opportunity for growth and transformation. We can choose to be swept away by the chaos, or we can learn to ride the waves with grace and resilience.

Imagine yourself standing on a shore, watching the waves crash against the rocks. Each wave is unique, bringing with it its own energy and force. Some are gentle, barely lapping at the shore, while others are powerful, crashing with thunderous force. This is a metaphor for change in our lives. Some changes are subtle, barely noticeable, while others are disruptive, shaking our foundations. The key to navigating this turbulent sea is to develop flexibility, resilience, and an open mind.

Flexibility is like a graceful dancer, effortlessly adapting to the rhythm of the music. It's about being able to adjust our plans, perspectives, and even our identities to accommodate the ebb and flow of change. Think of a tree that bends with the wind. Its roots dig deep into the ground, providing stability, while its branches sway gently, allowing it to withstand the storm. We can be like that tree, strong and flexible, able to bend without breaking.

Resilience is our inner strength, the ability to bounce back from setbacks and challenges. It's about finding our footing after we've been knocked down, dusting ourselves off, and moving forward with renewed determination. Think of a rubber band. When stretched to its limits, it may snap, but it always returns to its original shape. We can be like that rubber band, strong and resilient, able to endure stress and strain.

An open mind is like a clear window, allowing us to see the world with fresh perspective. It's about being open to new ideas, different viewpoints, and unexpected possibilities. Think of a child who sees the world with wonder and curiosity. They ask questions, explore, and learn without judgment or preconceived notions. We can be like that child, curious and open-minded, eager to learn and grow.

Here are some practical strategies for adapting to change and navigating uncertainty:

- **Embrace the Unknown:** Fear of the unknown is a powerful force that can paralyze us and prevent us from embracing change. However, it's important to remember that every change, no matter how daunting, presents an opportunity for growth and discovery. Embrace the unknown with a sense of adventure and curiosity.

- **Challenge Your Beliefs:** Our beliefs shape our perceptions of the world and influence our responses to change. When faced with a new situation, take a moment to examine your beliefs about it. Are they limiting or empowering? If they are limiting, challenge them and replace them with beliefs that support your growth and flexibility.

- **Practice Mindfulness:** Mindfulness is the art of being present in the moment, observing your thoughts and feelings without judgment. When you are mindful, you are more aware of your reactions to change and better able to manage them. Practice mindfulness through meditation, deep breathing exercises, or simply focusing on your senses.

- **Develop a Growth Mindset:** A growth mindset is the belief that our abilities and intelligence can be developed through effort and learning. Those with a growth mindset see challenges as opportunities for growth and are more resilient in the face of setbacks. Cultivate a growth mindset by embracing learning, seeking feedback, and challenging yourself to step outside your comfort zone.

- **Build a Support System:** Surrounding yourself with positive and supportive people can make a world of difference when navigating change. Find friends, family members, or mentors who encourage your growth, offer support during difficult times, and celebrate your successes.

- **Focus on Your Strengths:** When faced with change, it's easy to get caught up in our weaknesses and limitations. However, it's important to focus on our strengths. Identify your unique skills, talents, and passions. By focusing on your strengths, you can build confidence and resilience in the face of challenges.

- **Embrace Imperfection:** Perfectionism is a recipe for stress and anxiety, especially during times of change. Accept that you won't always get things right, and that's okay. Embrace your imperfections and learn from your mistakes.

- **Be Kind to Yourself:** Change can be stressful, and it's important to be kind to yourself during this time. Give yourself permission to feel your emotions without judgment. Practice self-compassion and celebrate your successes, no matter how small.

Remember, change is a constant in life, and it's something we can learn to navigate with grace and resilience. By embracing the unknown, challenging our beliefs, practicing mindfulness, and focusing on our strengths, we can not only adapt to change but also thrive in its midst.

The journey of change is not always easy, but it's an opportunity for growth, discovery, and transformation. Embrace the unknown, be open to new possibilities, and believe in your ability to navigate the challenges with grace and resilience. The rewards are well worth the effort, and the journey itself will be a testament to your strength and adaptability.

Overcoming Resistance to Change

Change is an inevitable part of life, like the changing seasons or the ebb and flow of the tides. It's a constant companion, guiding us through life's adventures and presenting us with opportunities for growth and transformation. But embracing change can be challenging. It often requires us to step outside our comfort zones, confront our fears, and let go of familiar patterns. This can be daunting, leading to resistance and a desire to cling to the known, even if it no longer serves us.

Think about it when was the last time you were presented with a new opportunity or faced a situation that required you to adapt? Did you feel a sense of excitement or perhaps a tinge of anxiety? Perhaps a mix of both? We all experience resistance to change in different ways. It might manifest as procrastination, avoidance, or even outright denial. We might find ourselves clinging to old habits, clinging to the past, or fearing the unknown.

Our resistance to change often stems from deeply ingrained fears. It's a natural human instinct to protect ourselves from perceived threats, and change can feel like a threat to our sense of security, identity, or control. Here are some common fears that contribute to resistance:

- **Fear of the unknown:** Change often involves stepping into uncharted territory, where the outcome is uncertain. This can be unsettling, as we crave predictability and control in our lives. The unknown can trigger our fear of failure, the fear of losing something we cherish, or the fear of not being good enough.

- **Fear of failure:** Change often requires us to take risks, and risks carry the potential for failure. This fear can paralyze us, making it difficult to embrace new opportunities or try new things. We fear the judgment of others, the potential disappointment, or the feeling of being inadequate.

- **Fear of losing control:** When we resist change, it's often because we feel a loss of control. We might fear losing our autonomy, our sense of purpose, or our position in life. The thought of relinquishing control can be frightening, making us cling to the familiar, even if it's no longer serving us.

- **Fear of the unknown:** This fear is a natural instinct to protect ourselves from perceived threats, and change can feel like a threat to our sense of security, identity, or control. It's our fear of the unknown that causes us to cling to the familiar, even if it's no longer serving us. The uncertainty of the future can be overwhelming, leading us to resist change and remain in our comfort zones, where we feel safe, even if we are unhappy.

- **Fear of rejection:** Embracing change often requires us to be vulnerable, to open ourselves up to new experiences and possibilities.

This can be intimidating, as we fear being rejected or judged by others. We worry about not being accepted, not being good enough, or not fitting in.

But just because we fear change doesn't mean we should avoid it. In fact, embracing change is essential for personal growth and fulfillment. Change is the catalyst for evolution, for transformation, and for unlocking our true potential.

Here are some effective techniques for overcoming resistance to change and embracing growth:

1. **Acknowledge and Embrace Your Fears:** The first step is to acknowledge the fears that are holding you back. Be honest with yourself about what's causing your resistance. Don't try to suppress or ignore your feelings. Instead, embrace them as a part of your human experience. Recognize that fear is a signal, not a stop sign. It's telling you something important, and it's crucial to understand its message. Once you understand your fears, you can start to address them.

2. **Challenge Your Negative Thoughts:** Once you've identified your fears, begin to challenge the negative thoughts that fuel them. Are your fears based on reality or are they simply assumptions? What evidence do you have to support your fears? Can you reframe your negative thoughts into more positive and empowering ones? For example, if you're afraid of failing, you can challenge that thought by asking yourself, "What's the worst that could happen? How likely is that to actually occur? What can I do to mitigate the risks?"

3. **Develop a Plan for Managing Fear:** Once you've acknowledged your fears and challenged your negative thoughts, you can create a plan for managing them. Start by breaking down the change into smaller,

manageable steps. This can make the process feel less overwhelming. Visualize yourself successfully navigating each step, and celebrate your progress along the way. Remember, even small steps forward can make a big difference.

4. **Embrace Uncertainty and Trust the Process:** Change is inherently uncertain, but that doesn't mean it's a bad thing. Embrace the unknown as an opportunity for growth and adventure. Trust in your ability to adapt and adjust, and remember that you are not alone in this journey. There are people who can support you, and resources available to help you navigate the challenges of change.

5. **Seek Support:** Don't try to go through this alone. Reach out to friends, family, mentors, or a therapist for support and guidance. Talking to someone you trust can help you process your fears, gain perspective, and feel more empowered.

6. **Practice Mindfulness and Self-Compassion:** During times of change, it's crucial to practice self-compassion and mindfulness. This means being kind and understanding toward yourself, even when you make mistakes or feel overwhelmed. Practice mindfulness to stay present in the moment and observe your thoughts and feelings without judgment. This can help you to manage anxiety and develop a more balanced perspective.

Remember, change is not something to be feared, but rather an opportunity for growth and transformation. It's a chance to redefine yourself, to discover new possibilities, and to create a life that is more fulfilling and authentic. By learning to overcome resistance to change, we can unlock our full potential and embrace a life of endless possibilities.

The journey of embracing change can be challenging, but it's also an adventure. It's a chance to rewrite your story, to create a narrative that is filled with growth, resilience, and ultimately, a deep sense of fulfillment. As you navigate the twists and turns of this journey, remember this: You are capable of far more than you realize. You have the strength to overcome any obstacle and the resilience to adapt to any change. Trust in yourself, embrace the process, and keep moving forward. The best is yet to come!

The Power of Stepping Outside Your Comfort Zone

Stepping outside your comfort zone is like venturing into uncharted territory, a journey that promises both exhilaration and trepidation. It's the act of pushing beyond familiar boundaries, embracing the unknown, and challenging yourself to grow. While it may feel daunting at first, the rewards of this courageous act are immeasurable. It's through these experiences, these calculated leaps of faith, that we truly discover our potential, build resilience, and unlock a deeper sense of fulfillment.

Imagine a seasoned mountain climber, accustomed to conquering treacherous peaks. One day, they decide to take on a new challenge, a climb that requires a different set of skills, a new approach. They face unfamiliar terrains, unpredictable weather, and the constant push of their own limitations. But with every step they take, they build strength, sharpen their instincts, and deepen their understanding of themselves and the world around them.

The same applies to every aspect of our lives. Stepping outside our comfort zone might mean trying a new hobby, taking a different route to work, or engaging in a conversation with someone we'd usually avoid. It could be as simple as ordering a dish we've never tried before or speaking up in a meeting. Each act, however small, represents a commitment to growth and a willingness to embrace the unknown.

The benefits of this practice are undeniable. By stepping outside our comfort zones, we learn to adapt to new situations, develop resilience in the face of challenges, and build confidence in our abilities. We break free from the shackles of fear and self-doubt, opening ourselves to a world of possibilities.

Stepping outside your comfort zone doesn't necessarily mean making drastic changes overnight. It's about taking small, incremental steps towards growth. Start by identifying areas where you feel a sense of discomfort or hesitation. Perhaps you're afraid of public speaking, hesitant to try a new sport, or apprehensive about asking for a promotion. Once you've identified these areas, start by setting small, achievable goals.

For example, if you're afraid of public speaking, start by practicing in front of a mirror, then in front of a small group of friends. Gradually work your way up to speaking in front of larger audiences. The key is to challenge yourself in manageable increments, building confidence and momentum along the way.

As you venture outside your comfort zone, you'll encounter setbacks and challenges. It's important to remember that failure is not the end but rather a stepping stone to growth. Embrace your mistakes as valuable lessons, learn from them, and keep moving forward. The more you challenge yourself, the more resilient you'll become.

Remember, stepping outside your comfort zone is not about achieving perfection or becoming fearless. It's about embracing the journey of growth, celebrating your successes, and learning from your mistakes. It's about recognizing that discomfort is a natural part of the process and that it can lead to profound personal transformation.

Embrace the unknown, push your boundaries, and watch as your confidence grows, your resilience deepens, and your potential unfolds. You'll discover that the most fulfilling experiences lie just beyond the edges of your comfort zone, waiting to be embraced.

Here are some practical tips for stepping outside your comfort zone:

- **Identify your comfort zone:** Take a moment to reflect on your daily routine and identify areas where you feel comfortable and areas where you feel a sense of hesitation or fear.

- **Set small, achievable goals:** Don't try to overhaul your entire life overnight. Start with small, manageable goals that will help you gradually push your boundaries.

- **Embrace the discomfort:** Remember that discomfort is a natural part of growth. Embrace it as a sign that you're challenging yourself and stepping outside your comfort zone.

- **Challenge your negative thoughts:** When faced with fear or doubt, challenge those negative thoughts and replace them with positive affirmations.

- **Celebrate your successes:** Acknowledge and celebrate your achievements, no matter how small they may seem.

- **Don't be afraid to ask for help:** Reach out to friends, family, or mentors for support and encouragement.

Stepping outside your comfort zone is a continuous process of learning, growth, and self-discovery. It's about embracing the unknown, pushing your boundaries, and discovering the limitless potential that lies within you. By committing to this practice, you'll unlock a life filled with greater confidence, resilience, and fulfillment. So, take that first step, however small it may seem, and watch as your journey of growth begins.

Continuous Growth and Transformation

Imagine a majestic oak tree, its roots firmly planted in the earth, its branches reaching towards the sky. Over time, it endures harsh winds, scorching sun, and pouring rain. Yet, it stands tall, adapting to the changing seasons, growing stronger with each passing year. Just like the oak tree, we too are constantly evolving, embracing life's challenges and transforming into our best selves.

Life is a continuous journey of growth and transformation. It's not a destination, but an ongoing process of learning, evolving, and becoming the best versions of ourselves. We are not static beings; we are dynamic, ever-changing individuals with the capacity to grow and learn throughout our lives.

Think back to your childhood. You were a sponge, absorbing information and experiences at an incredible pace. You learned to walk, talk, and interact with the world around you. Each milestone, each new skill, marked a significant step in your personal growth.

As we navigate the complexities of adulthood, the journey of growth continues. We encounter new challenges, face setbacks, and discover hidden strengths within ourselves. We experience heartbreak and joy, failures and triumphs. Each experience, no matter how big or small, leaves an imprint on our souls, shaping us into the individuals we are today.

The key to unlocking continuous growth lies in our willingness to embrace change and learn from our experiences. It's about recognizing that personal growth is not a linear path; it's a winding road with unexpected twists and turns. Sometimes, we might feel lost, confused, or even stagnant. But remember, even the most challenging periods can be opportunities for profound transformation.

Embracing change requires a shift in perspective. It means seeing challenges not as obstacles, but as opportunities for growth. It's about viewing setbacks as stepping stones on our path to success. When we adopt this mindset, we empower ourselves to overcome adversity and emerge stronger on the other side.

Growth often occurs outside of our comfort zones. It's in those moments of vulnerability, when we push our limits and challenge our preconceived notions, that we truly expand our horizons. It's about embracing the unknown, stepping into the unfamiliar, and allowing ourselves to evolve.

Imagine a sculptor working with a block of raw marble. They don't just chip away at the stone; they carefully shape it, revealing its inner beauty. Each stroke of the chisel, each deliberate cut, transforms the raw material into a masterpiece. Similarly, our lives are works in progress. With every experience, every challenge we overcome, we shape ourselves into something more beautiful, more resilient, and more fulfilling.

Here are some practical tips to cultivate a mindset of continuous growth and transformation:

- **Embrace a growth mindset:** Believe that you are capable of learning, evolving, and improving throughout your life. Embrace challenges as opportunities for growth and learning.

- **Seek out new experiences:** Step outside of your comfort zone and engage in activities that push your boundaries. This can be anything from taking a new class to traveling to a new destination.

- **Reflect on your experiences:** Take time to reflect on your experiences and identify areas where you can grow. Journaling, meditation, and conversations with trusted friends can be helpful tools for self-reflection.

- **Set goals and pursue your passions:** Having clear goals and pursuing your passions provides a sense of direction and purpose in your life. This keeps you motivated and engaged in the journey of growth.

- **Embrace failure as a learning opportunity:** Don't be afraid to make mistakes. Every failure is an opportunity to learn and grow. Analyze your mistakes, identify areas for improvement, and move forward with renewed determination.

- **Practice self-compassion:** Treat yourself with kindness and understanding. Acknowledge your strengths and celebrate your accomplishments, while also accepting your imperfections.

- **Surround yourself with supportive people:** Build a network of friends, family, and mentors who encourage your growth and provide positive support.

The journey of continuous growth is a lifelong endeavor. It's about embracing change, challenging ourselves, and continually striving to become the best versions of ourselves. It's about recognizing that life is not about reaching a certain destination, but about the journey itself.

Imagine a river, flowing steadily towards the sea. It encounters rocks, rapids, and winding paths, yet it continues to flow, always moving forward. Just like the river, we too are in constant motion. We are constantly adapting, evolving, and growing. Embrace this journey of continuous growth and transformation, for it is in this process that we truly come alive.

CHAPTER 12

THE POWER OF CONNECTION AND COMMUNITY

The Importance of Belonging

Imagine a tiny seed, planted deep within the earth, yearning to reach for the sun. It craves nourishment, warmth, and connection to thrive. Just like that seed, humans have a deep-seated longing for belonging, a fundamental need to connect with others and feel a sense of acceptance and purpose. This innate desire to be part of something larger than ourselves drives us to seek out communities and social groups that resonate with our values, passions, and aspirations.

Throughout our lives, we encounter a diverse array of communities families, neighborhoods, schools, workplaces, religious institutions, sports teams, and countless others. These groups provide us with a sense of identity, purpose, and belonging, shaping our experiences and contributing to our overall well-being.

Imagine a child growing up in a loving family. The unwavering support, encouragement, and shared traditions create a foundation of security and belonging. These early experiences lay the groundwork for healthy emotional development and a sense of self-worth. Later in life, as we venture beyond our families, we seek out friendships and social connections that nurture our hearts and minds.

The importance of belonging extends far beyond emotional fulfillment. Communities and social groups play a crucial role in supporting our physical and mental health. When we feel connected to others, we are less likely to experience loneliness, depression, and anxiety. Studies have shown that strong social connections can boost our immune systems, improve our cardiovascular health, and even increase our lifespan.

Beyond individual well-being, communities also serve as vital pillars of society, fostering collaboration, problem-solving, and a sense of shared responsibility. When people feel a sense of belonging to their communities, they are more likely to participate in civic activities, volunteer their time, and advocate for positive change.

However, in today's increasingly interconnected world, it can be easy to feel disconnected and isolated. The rise of social media and virtual communication, while providing avenues for connection, can sometimes create a false sense of belonging, leaving us feeling more isolated than ever.

Many factors contribute to this disconnect. Urbanization, globalization, and the rapid pace of change can leave individuals feeling uprooted and disconnected from their roots. The pressure to succeed, the pursuit of individual goals, and the constant bombardment of information can make it challenging to cultivate meaningful connections.

The good news is that despite these challenges, the human spirit yearns for connection. We are hardwired to seek out belonging, and there are numerous ways to cultivate it in our lives.

The first step is to identify what truly matters to you. What are your passions, values, and interests? What kind of community do you envision yourself belonging to? Once you have a clear understanding of your needs and desires, you can actively seek out opportunities for connection.

Join clubs, volunteer organizations, or community groups that align with your interests. Participate in local events, festivals, or workshops. Attend gatherings that bring people together with shared passions, such as book clubs, hiking groups, or art classes.

Remember, building meaningful connections takes time and effort. Be patient, be open-minded, and be willing to step outside of your comfort zone. Engage in conversations, listen attentively, and be genuinely interested in getting to know others.

As you cultivate connections, you'll discover that you are not alone in your journey. You'll find support, encouragement, and a sense of purpose within a community of like-minded individuals.

Building a strong sense of belonging is an ongoing process, but it is a rewarding and enriching one. As you connect with others, you'll not only find a sense of purpose and fulfillment but also contribute to a more interconnected and supportive world.

Finding Your Tribe

Imagine a bustling marketplace, vibrant with energy and filled with diverse stalls showcasing unique wares. Each stall represents a different interest, a different passion, a different way of seeing the world. Now picture yourself entering this marketplace, not to buy goods, but to find your tribe - a group of people who share your values, your interests, your vision.

This is the essence of finding your tribe. It's about surrounding yourself with individuals who resonate with your core values and who see the world in a way similar to yours. It's about finding a community where you feel understood, supported, and encouraged to be your authentic self.

In today's world, where we're bombarded with endless messages and bombarded with information, it's easy to feel isolated and disconnected. The noise of the world can drown out our own inner voice, making it difficult to find a sense of belonging. But finding your tribe can be a powerful antidote to this sense of isolation.

Think of it like finding your home away from home. Your tribe becomes a safe haven, a place where you can be yourself without judgment, where you can share your hopes and fears, and where you can learn and grow alongside others who are on a similar journey.

But how do you find this tribe? Where do you begin your search for these kindred spirits?

The first step is to identify your interests and passions. What are you naturally drawn to? What activities energize you and bring you joy? What causes are you passionate about? Once you have a clear understanding of your interests, you can start exploring groups, organizations, or communities that align with your values.

Think about the things that you enjoy doing in your free time. Are you passionate about sports, music, art, writing, or technology? Are you drawn to social justice, environmental issues, or animal welfare?

Perhaps you're interested in learning new skills or exploring different cultures. Maybe you're drawn to spiritual practices or community service. There are countless ways to connect with people who share your passions, so don't be afraid to step outside of your comfort zone and explore new avenues.

One of the most powerful ways to find your tribe is to get involved in activities that you enjoy. Join a sports team, take a dance class, volunteer at a local charity, or start a book club. Participating in activities that align with your interests will not only introduce you to like-minded individuals but also allow you to build meaningful connections based on shared passions.

Another way to find your tribe is to use online platforms and social media. There are numerous groups, forums, and online communities dedicated to almost every interest imaginable. These platforms can be a great way to connect with people who share your values, even if you're geographically distant.

But remember, finding your tribe isn't just about finding people who share your interests. It's also about finding people who are supportive, encouraging, and positive. You want to surround yourself with individuals who uplift you, challenge you to grow, and celebrate your successes.

Look for people who inspire you, who are passionate about their lives, and who are always striving to learn and grow. Surround yourself with individuals who offer constructive feedback, who are willing to listen to your concerns, and who are always there to cheer you on.

Here are some tips for finding your tribe:

1. **Be Open and Approachable:** Don't be afraid to strike up conversations with people who share your interests. Be open to meeting new people and forming new connections.

2. **Attend Events and Workshops:** Participate in events and workshops related to your passions. This will allow you to meet like-minded individuals who are also interested in learning and growing.

3. **Join Online Communities:** Explore online platforms and social media groups that cater to your interests. These can be great resources for connecting with people from around the world.

4. **Volunteer Your Time:** Volunteering is a fantastic way to connect with others who are passionate about making a difference. You'll meet people who are compassionate, driven, and committed to making the world a better place.

5. **Be Authentic:** Be true to yourself and don't try to fit in. If you're passionate about something, embrace it and don't be afraid to share it with the world.

6. **Be Patient and Persistent:** Finding your tribe takes time and effort. Don't get discouraged if you don't find it immediately. Keep searching, keep networking, and keep putting yourself out there.

The power of connection and community is undeniable. Surrounding yourself with positive and supportive people can have a profound impact on your overall well-being, your personal growth, and your ability to achieve your goals.

Remember, you're not alone on your journey of self-discovery and personal growth. Find your tribe, connect with like-minded individuals, and create a community that supports and empowers you to be your best self.

Contributing to Your Community

You see, contributing to your community is like planting seeds. You may not see the fruit of your labor immediately, but over time, it can blossom into something beautiful and impactful. It's a two-way street that enriches both you and the people around you.

Imagine yourself walking through a bustling city, where the streets are lined with vibrant shops and friendly faces. There's a certain energy that permeates the air, a sense of community that binds everyone together. Now, picture yourself in a quiet town where the pace of life is slower and the connections between people are deeper. You can feel the warmth of shared stories and experiences that have woven a rich tapestry of history and tradition.

Both these scenarios offer a glimpse into the power of community. It's that invisible thread that connects us, that reminds us that we're not alone in this journey called life. But it's not just about feeling connected; it's also about actively participating in making a difference.

Think about the times you've received help, support, or kindness from someone else. Maybe a friend offered a listening ear when you were going through a difficult time, or a stranger held the door open for you. These small acts of generosity, no matter how insignificant they might seem, have a ripple effect that spreads far beyond the initial interaction.

Now, imagine yourself on the other side of that coin. You're the one offering a helping hand, a listening ear, or a smile of encouragement. This is the essence of contributing to your community. It's about recognizing that your actions, however big or small, can leave a lasting mark on the world around you.

Volunteering is one of the most powerful ways to contribute to your community. Picture yourself spending an afternoon at a local soup kitchen, serving meals to those in need. Or perhaps you're mentoring a young child, guiding them on their educational journey. You might be involved in cleaning up a local park, ensuring that it remains a beautiful and welcoming space for everyone to enjoy.

These acts of service may not always be glamorous, but they are deeply rewarding. You get to witness firsthand the impact you're making on the lives of others, and it fills your heart with a sense of purpose and fulfillment that's truly unmatched.

Volunteering is not just about giving back; it's also about discovering new skills and expanding your horizons. Imagine yourself joining a community garden, learning about sustainable gardening practices and connecting with nature in a whole new way. Or perhaps you're volunteering at a local animal shelter, caring for abandoned pets and experiencing the unconditional love they offer.

These experiences open your eyes to different perspectives and challenge you to step outside of your comfort zone. They cultivate empathy, compassion, and a sense of shared humanity that enriches your own life in countless ways.

But contributing to your community doesn't have to be limited to formal volunteer work. You can make a difference in countless small ways. Consider offering a helping hand to a neighbor who's struggling with their groceries or simply taking the time to listen to a friend who needs someone to talk to. You can even leave a positive review for a local business that has provided exceptional service.

These seemingly insignificant actions, when combined with the collective efforts of others, create a ripple effect that can transform communities. They foster a sense of belonging, shared responsibility, and collective well-being that benefits everyone involved.

Think of your community as a vibrant tapestry woven together by the threads of individual contributions. Each act of kindness, each moment of support, and each effort to make a difference adds a new thread, strengthening the overall fabric of your community.

As you embark on your journey of self-discovery and personal growth, remember that the most fulfilling and meaningful life is often one that extends beyond yourself. By contributing to your community, you not only make a positive impact on the world around you, but you also enrich your own life in ways you may never have imagined.

The beauty of contributing to your community lies in the fact that it's a journey of continuous learning and growth. You'll constantly discover new ways to make a difference, new opportunities to connect with others, and new reasons to feel grateful for the gift of belonging.

So, the next time you're feeling a little lost or unfulfilled, consider stepping outside of your comfort zone and making a difference in your community. It might just be the spark you need to ignite a fire within, reminding you of your own potential and the power you have to create a better world for yourself and others.

You have the power to choose how you want to live your life. You can choose to be a passive observer or an active participant in creating a better world. The choice is yours, and the possibilities are endless.

Remember, the most fulfilling and meaningful life is one that is lived in connection with others. By contributing to your community, you're not only enriching the lives of others, but you're also enriching your own.

Go forth and make a difference! The world needs your unique talents and contributions. You have the power to create a brighter future, one act of kindness at a time.

Building Meaningful Connections

The ability to connect with others is an essential aspect of human existence. It enriches our lives, brings us joy, and provides us with a sense of belonging. In today's fast-paced world, however, it's easy to feel disconnected and isolated.

We spend hours glued to our screens, scrolling through social media feeds, and often neglect the vital need for genuine human interaction.

Building meaningful connections is not about accumulating a vast network of acquaintances; it's about cultivating deep, authentic relationships that nourish our souls. It's about finding people who understand us, support us, and inspire us to grow.

Think of it this way: Imagine a lush, vibrant garden. Each plant represents a different person in our lives. To nurture a thriving garden, we must provide each plant with the right amount of sunlight, water, and nutrients. Similarly, to foster meaningful connections, we need to actively cultivate them.

The first step towards building meaningful connections is to be present. In a world filled with distractions, it's easy to get caught up in our own thoughts and miss what's happening around us. To truly connect with someone, we need to put our phones away, make eye contact, and listen attentively. This is where the art of active listening comes in.

Active listening is more than just hearing words; it's about understanding the speaker's emotions, intentions, and perspectives. It involves paying attention to their body language, tone of voice, and the subtle nuances of their communication. It's about engaging with their story, asking clarifying questions, and showing genuine interest in what they have to say.

Imagine you're sitting across from a friend who's sharing a difficult experience. Instead of simply nodding and waiting for your turn to speak, you lean in, make eye contact, and ask open-ended questions that encourage them to elaborate. You might say, "Tell me more about that," or "What were you feeling at that moment?" By showing genuine interest and empathy, you create a safe space for them to share their feelings and feel heard.

Empathy is another crucial element in building meaningful connections. It's the ability to understand and share another person's feelings, even if we don't fully agree with their perspective. When we practice empathy, we step outside of ourselves and try to see the world through their eyes. It's about acknowledging their emotions, validating their experiences, and showing compassion.

Imagine a coworker who's struggling with a stressful project. Instead of dismissing their concerns, you take the time to listen to their frustrations and offer words of support. You might say, "I can see you're feeling overwhelmed. Is there anything I can do to help?" By demonstrating empathy, you show that you care and create a connection based on understanding and support.

Beyond active listening and empathy, genuine interest is essential for building meaningful connections. It's about showing that you care about the other person, their thoughts, feelings, and experiences. It's about wanting to learn more about them, their hobbies, passions, and dreams.

Think of it like a conversation with a friend. Instead of simply waiting for your turn to speak, you ask questions that show you're genuinely interested in what they have to say. You might ask about their recent trip, a book they're reading, or a project they're working on. By showing genuine interest, you create a sense of connection that fosters intimacy and trust.

Imagine you're at a networking event and meeting someone who works in a field that interests you. Instead of focusing solely on your own achievements, you ask questions about their work, their experiences, and their goals. You might say, "What drew you to this field?" or "What are some of the biggest challenges you've faced?" By expressing genuine interest, you not only learn something new but also create a connection that can potentially lead to a valuable friendship or collaboration.

Remember, building meaningful connections is a two-way street. It requires effort, patience, and a willingness to be vulnerable. It's about being present, listening actively, practicing empathy, and showing genuine interest. When we invest in our relationships, we enrich our lives and create a network of support that can help us navigate the challenges and celebrate the triumphs of life.

The Power of Shared Experiences

Think back to your favorite memories, the ones that make your heart swell with warmth and nostalgia. Are they mostly solo adventures, or do they involve shared laughter, whispered secrets, and the comfort of connection? The truth is some of the most profound moments in life are woven with the threads of shared experiences.

We are social creatures, inherently wired for connection. These connections are more than just fleeting encounters; they are the foundations upon which we build a sense of belonging, understanding, and purpose. Shared experiences are the bricks and mortar that cement these connections, building bridges of trust and empathy.

Imagine two strangers meeting at a bustling farmers market. One offers the other a taste of their locally sourced honey, and a conversation sparks. They share stories about their gardens, their families, their hopes for the future. This seemingly insignificant interaction becomes a foundation for a deeper connection – a shared experience that binds them together.

As we delve deeper into shared experiences, we discover their profound impact on our personal growth and emotional well-being. They offer us:

- **A Sense of Belonging:** When we share laughter and tears with others, we create a sense of belonging, a recognition that we are not alone in this world. These shared moments of vulnerability and connection strengthen our bonds, reminding us that we are part of a larger community.

- **A Deeper Understanding:** Through shared experiences, we gain a deeper understanding of ourselves and others. We witness different perspectives, learn from diverse backgrounds, and discover the beauty of human connection.

- **A Source of Strength:** In times of difficulty, our shared experiences become a source of strength and resilience. We draw upon the support and encouragement of others, knowing that we have weathered storms together and can face future challenges with confidence.

- **A Tapestry of Memories:** The memories woven from shared experiences are priceless treasures. They serve as reminders of the joys, challenges, and triumphs we have shared with those we love. They offer us a sense of continuity and purpose, anchoring us to the past and fueling our journey forward.

How can we cultivate more shared experiences in our lives? It starts by embracing the simple joys of connection.

Here are some practical ideas:

- **Join a book club or a hiking group:** Sharing a passion for literature or nature with others can be a wonderful way to forge new connections and create lasting memories.

- **Volunteer at a local organization:** Giving back to your community is not only a fulfilling experience but also a great way to connect with people who share your values and desire to make a difference.

- **Attend community events:** From festivals to concerts to art exhibitions, community events are designed to bring people together and create shared experiences.

- **Organize a potluck dinner or a game night with friends and family:** Sharing a meal or a game is a simple yet powerful way to foster connection and create lasting memories.

- **Start a new hobby or take a class with a friend:** Learning a new skill together can be both challenging and rewarding, strengthening your bond and creating shared experiences.

- **Travel with loved ones:** Whether it's a weekend getaway or a longer adventure, traveling together creates opportunities to explore new cultures, overcome challenges, and forge unforgettable memories.

- **Simply engage in conversations with those around you:** Don't underestimate the power of genuine conversations. Listening attentively, sharing your thoughts and experiences, and connecting with others on a deeper level can create meaningful connections.

Remember, the most impactful shared experiences are not about the grandeur of the event, but the depth of the connection. A simple conversation over a cup of coffee, a shared laugh during a walk in the park, or a helping hand offered during a challenging time can weave powerful threads in the tapestry of your life.

Embracing shared experiences is not merely about having fun; it's about cultivating a richer, more meaningful life. It's about weaving a web of connections that provide support, understanding, and a sense of belonging in a world that can sometimes feel isolating. So, step out of your comfort zone, embrace the opportunities for connection, and embark on a journey of shared experiences that will enrich your life in countless ways.

CHAPTER 13

THE ROLE OF MINDFULNESS AND MEDITATION

The Benefits of Mindfulness

Imagine a world where you can navigate the choppy waters of life with a calm and steady mind. A world where you can meet challenges head-on, not with fear and anxiety, but with clarity and focus. This is the promise of mindfulness, a practice that has been cultivated for centuries and is now gaining widespread recognition for its profound benefits.

Mindfulness is essentially about paying attention, in the present moment, without judgment. It's about becoming aware of your thoughts, feelings, and sensations without getting carried away by them. It's like stepping back from the whirlwind of your mind and observing it with a sense of detachment.

Think of it like this: Imagine you're walking through a bustling city. There are cars honking, people chattering, and a million things vying for your attention. But you're able to walk calmly through the chaos, noticing it all without letting it overwhelm you. You're present, aware, and grounded. That's mindfulness in action.

But what are the practical benefits of this practice? Why should you bother cultivating mindfulness in your busy life? The answer lies in the profound impact it has on your mental and emotional well-being.

Stress Reduction: A Calm in the Storm

In today's fast-paced world, stress has become almost a constant companion. We're bombarded with deadlines, responsibilities, and a constant stream of information. This constant pressure can take a toll on our mental and physical health. Mindfulness offers a powerful antidote to this stress epidemic.

By focusing on the present moment, mindfulness helps us detach from the worries and anxieties of the future, and the regrets and frustrations of the past. It allows us to experience a sense of peace and calm, even amidst the storm of life's challenges.

Think about it: When you're caught up in the cycle of worry, your mind races with endless "what ifs" and "should haves." This constant stream of negative thoughts can lead to physical symptoms like tension headaches, muscle aches, and digestive problems. But mindfulness helps you break free from this cycle. By focusing on your breath, your body, and the present moment, you interrupt the flow of negative thoughts and create space for a sense of calm and ease.

Numerous studies have shown that mindfulness practices like meditation can reduce stress hormones like cortisol, leading to lower blood pressure and heart rate. This, in turn, can improve your overall health and well-being.

Improved Focus: A Clearer Mind

In a world of constant distractions, maintaining focus can be a real challenge. Whether you're trying to concentrate at work, study for an exam, or simply enjoy a peaceful moment, distractions can easily derail your attention. But mindfulness can help you train your mind to stay focused.

By cultivating mindfulness, you become more aware of your thoughts and sensations, and you learn to identify and let go of distractions. This allows you to focus your attention more effectively, whether it's on a specific task, a conversation, or simply the beauty of your surroundings.

Imagine trying to read a book while your mind is filled with worries about upcoming deadlines or unfinished chores. It's nearly impossible to truly engage with the text. But with mindfulness, you can train your mind to let go of those distractions and immerse yourself in the present moment. You become more attentive, more engaged, and more capable of absorbing information.

This improved focus translates into better performance in all areas of your life. Whether you're at work, school, or simply trying to enjoy a peaceful evening, mindfulness can help you stay present and engaged.

Enhanced Self-Awareness: Knowing Yourself Better

Mindfulness is not just about calming your mind and improving your focus; it's also about deepening your self-awareness. By paying attention to your thoughts, feelings, and sensations, you gain a deeper understanding of yourself. You become more aware of your emotional triggers, your thought patterns, and your reactions to different situations.

This increased self-awareness allows you to make more conscious choices in your life. You become more aware of your habits, both positive and negative, and you gain the ability to make changes that align with your values and goals.

Imagine you're struggling with a recurring negative thought pattern. Mindfulness helps you become aware of this pattern and notice the thoughts as they arise, without judgment. This awareness gives you the power to challenge these thoughts and replace them with more positive and empowering ones.

Mindfulness in Action: Bringing It into Your Daily Life

You don't need to spend hours in meditation retreats to experience the benefits of mindfulness. You can easily incorporate mindfulness into your daily life through simple practices. Here are a few ideas:

- **Mindful Breathing:** Find a quiet spot where you can sit comfortably. Close your eyes and focus on your breath. Notice the rise and fall of your chest as you inhale and exhale. If your mind wanders, gently bring it back to your breath.

- **Body Scan Meditation:** Lie down or sit comfortably. Bring your attention to your body, starting with your toes. Notice any sensations, such as warmth, tingling, or pressure. Slowly scan your body from head to toe, paying attention to each part without judgment.

- **Mindful Walking:** As you walk, focus on the sensations of your feet on the ground, the movement of your legs, and the rhythm of your breath. Notice your surroundings, but without getting distracted by them.

- **Mindful Eating:** Before you eat, take a moment to appreciate the food in front of you. Notice its colors, textures, and smells. As you eat, savor each bite, paying attention to the flavors and sensations in your mouth.

- **Mindful Listening:** When you're in a conversation, focus on the speaker's words and their tone of voice. Try to understand their perspective and listen with empathy, rather than interrupting or formulating your response.

Building a Mindfulness Practice: Starting Small

The key to cultivating a successful mindfulness practice is to start small and be consistent. Even a few minutes of mindful breathing or body scan meditation each day can make a difference.

Here are some tips for getting started:

- **Find a Quiet Space:** Choose a comfortable and quiet place where you won't be interrupted.
- **Set a Timer:** Start with just 5 or 10 minutes of practice. You can gradually increase the duration as you become more comfortable.
- **Be Patient and Kind:** Don't get discouraged if your mind wanders. Just gently bring your attention back to your breath or your body.
- **Make It a Habit:** Try to practice mindfulness daily, even if it's just for a few minutes. Consistency is key to developing a strong mindfulness practice.
- **Explore Different Practices:** Experiment with different mindfulness techniques to find what works best for you.

Conclusion: Embracing the Power of Presence

Mindfulness is not just a trend; it's a powerful tool for improving your mental and emotional well-being. By cultivating awareness in the present moment, you can reduce stress, improve your focus, enhance your self-awareness, and live a more fulfilling life.

So take a deep breath, find a quiet spot, and begin your journey into the world of mindfulness. You might be surprised by the transformation it brings to your life.

Introduction to Meditation

Meditation is a practice that has been around for centuries, originating from ancient Eastern traditions. It involves focusing your attention on a single point, such as your breath, a mantra, or an image, and letting go of distracting thoughts. The goal is to achieve a state of deep relaxation and mental clarity.

There are many different types of meditation, each with its own unique approach and benefits. Some common types include:

- **Mindfulness Meditation:** This type of meditation involves paying attention to the present moment without judgment. You observe your thoughts, feelings, and sensations as they arise, without getting caught up in them. Mindfulness meditation is a great way to cultivate awareness and reduce stress.

- **Transcendental Meditation (TM):** This technique involves repeating a specific mantra silently to yourself, which helps quiet the mind and reduce mental chatter. TM is known for its stress-reducing effects and its ability to promote relaxation and inner peace.

- **Progressive Muscle Relaxation:** This technique involves systematically tensing and relaxing different muscle groups in your body. By focusing on the physical sensations of tension and relaxation, you can reduce stress and improve your overall sense of well-being.

- **Guided Meditation:** This type of meditation involves listening to a guided audio or video that leads you through a series of relaxation techniques and visualizations. Guided meditations can be helpful for reducing stress, improving sleep, and fostering a sense of peace.

- **Walking Meditation:** This practice involves bringing mindfulness to your walks, paying attention to the sensations of your feet on the ground, the movement of your body, and the surrounding environment. Walking meditation is a great way to connect with your body and experience the present moment.

- **Loving-Kindness Meditation:** This practice involves cultivating feelings of love, compassion, and kindness towards yourself and others. You can practice loving-kindness meditation by repeating phrases or mantras that express these feelings.

Benefits of Meditation:

Meditation has been shown to have a wide range of benefits for both physical and mental health. These benefits include:

- **Reduced Stress and Anxiety:** Meditation helps to calm the nervous system and reduce the production of stress hormones. This can lead to a reduction in feelings of anxiety, worry, and overwhelm.

- **Improved Sleep:** Regular meditation can help to regulate sleep patterns and improve sleep quality. It promotes relaxation and reduces racing thoughts that can interfere with falling asleep.

- **Increased Focus and Concentration:** By training your mind to stay present and focused, meditation can improve your attention span and your ability to concentrate on tasks.

- **Enhanced Emotional Regulation:** Meditation can help you to become more aware of your emotions and develop greater control over your emotional responses. This can help you to manage difficult feelings more effectively and reduce impulsiveness.

- **Greater Self-Awareness:** By quieting the mind and observing your thoughts and feelings without judgment, meditation can help you to gain a deeper understanding of yourself.

- **Improved Cardiovascular Health:** Studies have shown that meditation can lower blood pressure and reduce the risk of heart disease.

- **Reduced Inflammation:** Meditation has been shown to reduce inflammation throughout the body, which can help to prevent chronic disease.

- **Increased Empathy and Compassion:** Cultivating feelings of love and kindness towards yourself and others through loving-kindness meditation can foster empathy and compassion.

- **Enhanced Creativity:** Meditation can quiet the mind and open up space for creative thinking and problem-solving.

Getting Started with Meditation:

If you're new to meditation, it can be helpful to start with a guided meditation or join a meditation class. Here are a few tips for getting started:

- **Choose a Quiet Place:** Find a quiet and comfortable space where you won't be disturbed.

- **Set a Timer:** Start with short meditation sessions (5-10 minutes) and gradually increase the duration as you become more comfortable.

- **Focus on Your Breath:** Pay attention to the rise and fall of your breath. You can also try counting your breaths to stay focused.

- **Let Go of Distracting Thoughts:** It's normal for thoughts to arise during meditation. Simply acknowledge the thoughts without judgment and gently guide your attention back to your breath or your chosen object of focus.

- **Be Patient and Consistent:** Meditation is a practice, and it takes time and consistency to experience its full benefits. Don't get discouraged if you find it challenging at first.

Incorporating Meditation into Your Daily Life:

Once you've established a meditation practice, you can begin to incorporate it into your daily life. Here are a few ideas:

- **Start Your Day with Meditation:** Meditation can help to set a calm and focused tone for your day.

- **Meditate Before Bed:** Meditation can help to calm your mind and prepare your body for sleep.

- **Take Short Breaks Throughout the Day:** Use meditation to de-stress and recharge during breaks at work or school.

- **Meditate While Walking:** Use walking meditation to bring mindfulness to your daily walks.

- **Meditate During Chores:** You can practice mindfulness while doing everyday chores, such as washing dishes or folding laundry.

Meditation is a powerful tool that can transform your life. By taking time for meditation each day, you can reduce stress, improve sleep, cultivate inner peace, and enhance your overall well-being.

Simple Mindfulness Techniques

Mindfulness is a powerful practice that involves paying attention to the present moment without judgment. It's about cultivating awareness of your thoughts, feelings, sensations, and surroundings without getting carried away by them. When you practice mindfulness, you learn to observe your experiences with a gentle and curious attitude, allowing you to become more present in your life and cultivate a greater sense of peace and well-being.

There are many different ways to practice mindfulness, but some simple techniques can be easily incorporated into your daily routine. These practices can help you develop a greater awareness of your mind and body, reduce stress, and cultivate a more positive outlook.

Body Scan Meditation

Body scan meditation is a simple yet powerful technique that involves bringing your attention to your physical body. You start by focusing on your breath, noticing the sensation of each inhale and exhale. Then, you slowly scan your body, starting with your toes and moving up to your head, paying attention to any sensations you experience. You may notice warmth, tingling, pressure, or tightness in different parts of your body. As you scan, try to observe these sensations without judgment or trying to change them.

To begin a body scan meditation:

1. **Find a comfortable position:** You can lie down, sit up, or even do it while walking. The key is to find a position where you can relax and focus without feeling uncomfortable.

2. **Focus on your breath:** Close your eyes and turn your attention to your breath. Notice the sensation of each inhale and exhale. Don't try to control your breath; just observe it naturally.

3. **Begin scanning:** Slowly bring your attention to your toes. Notice any sensations you feel in your toes, such as warmth, tingling, pressure, or tightness.

4. **Move slowly upwards:** Gradually shift your attention to the soles of your feet, then your ankles, your calves, your knees, and so on. Continue scanning your entire body, moving slowly and paying attention to any sensations you feel.

5. **Observe without judgment:** As you scan your body, simply observe any sensations you experience without judgment or trying to change them. If you notice your mind wandering, gently guide it back to your body.

6. **Repeat the process:** You can repeat the body scan meditation for as long as you like, even just for a few minutes at a time.

Mindful Breathing Exercises

Mindful breathing exercises are a great way to bring your attention to the present moment and calm your mind. There are many different breathing exercises you can try, but the basic principle is to focus on your breath and observe the sensations of each inhale and exhale.

Here are a few simple breathing exercises you can try:

- **Box Breathing:** Imagine a square divided into four equal sides. Inhale slowly for four counts, hold your breath for four counts, exhale slowly for four counts, and hold your breath for four counts. Repeat this cycle for several minutes.

- **Diaphragmatic Breathing:** Place one hand on your chest and the other on your stomach. Inhale slowly and deeply, allowing your stomach to expand as you fill your lungs with air. Exhale slowly and completely, allowing your stomach to deflate. Repeat this cycle for several minutes.

- **Counting Breaths:** Inhale and mentally count to four, exhale and mentally count to four. Repeat this cycle for several minutes, focusing on the sensations of your breath.

- **Alternating Nostril Breathing:** Close your right nostril with your right thumb and inhale slowly through your left nostril. Close your left nostril with your right ring finger and exhale slowly through your right nostril. Inhale slowly through your right nostril, close your right nostril with your thumb, and exhale slowly through your left nostril. Repeat this cycle for several minutes.

Mindful Walking

Mindful walking is a great way to bring mindfulness into your daily routine. It involves paying close attention to the sensations of walking, such as the feeling of your feet on the ground, the movement of your legs, and the rhythm of your steps. You can practice mindful walking anywhere, whether it's on a trail, in a park, or even around your house.

To practice mindful walking:

1. **Choose a comfortable place:** Find a place where you can walk without distractions and feel safe.

2. **Start slowly:** Begin by taking a few slow, deliberate steps, paying attention to the feeling of your feet on the ground.

3. **Focus on your senses:** As you walk, notice the sensations of your body, such as the movement of your legs, the feeling of the wind on your skin, and the sounds around you.

4. **Observe without judgment:** Notice these sensations without judging them. Just let them be.

5. **Keep walking:** Continue walking at a comfortable pace, staying present in your body and your surroundings.

6. **Expand your awareness:** As you become more comfortable with mindful walking, you can start to expand your awareness to include your thoughts and emotions. Notice any thoughts that arise without getting carried away by them. Simply acknowledge them and let them go.

Integrating Mindfulness into Your Daily Life

Mindfulness is not a one-time event, but a practice that you can incorporate into your daily life. You can start by choosing one or two simple mindfulness techniques to practice regularly. Here are some ideas:

- **Start your day with mindful breathing:** Before you get out of bed, take a few minutes to practice mindful breathing. Focus on your breath and observe the sensations of each inhale and exhale. This can help you start your day feeling calm and centered.

- **Practice mindful eating:** When you eat, pay attention to the taste, texture, and aroma of your food. Savor each bite and enjoy the experience of eating. This can help you appreciate your meals more and prevent overeating.

- **Engage in mindful walking or exercise:** Take a few minutes each day to go for a mindful walk or engage in some form of mindful exercise. Focus on your body and your breath, noticing the sensations of movement and the feeling of the wind or sun on your skin.

- **Take mindful breaks throughout the day:** When you feel overwhelmed or stressed, take a few minutes to step away from what you're doing and practice mindful breathing or body scan meditation. This can help you calm your mind and refocus your attention.

- **Be present in conversations:** When you're talking with someone, pay attention to what they're saying and how they're saying it. Listen with genuine interest and try to understand their perspective. This can help you build stronger connections with others.

Cultivating a Mindful Lifestyle

By incorporating mindfulness into your daily life, you can begin to cultivate a more mindful lifestyle. This means being present in each moment, observing your experiences with a gentle and curious attitude, and responding to life's challenges with greater awareness and compassion.

As you practice mindfulness, you may notice some positive changes in your life. You may find that you're less reactive to stress, more focused, more compassionate, and more at ease with yourself and the world around you.

Mindfulness is a journey, not a destination. It's a practice that requires patience, persistence, and a willingness to be present in each moment. By embracing mindfulness, you can create a more fulfilling and joyful life.

The Power of Gratitude Meditation

Gratitude meditation is a powerful practice that can shift your focus to the positive aspects of life, fostering happiness and well-being. Imagine yourself walking through a bustling city, bombarded with sights, sounds, and a constant stream of information. It's easy to get caught up in the rush, focusing on what's lacking or what needs to be fixed. Gratitude meditation acts like a gentle reminder to pause, breathe, and appreciate the good things in your life, even amidst the chaos.

The practice involves taking a few moments each day to reflect on the things you are grateful for. It's not about ignoring the challenges or pretending they don't exist; it's about intentionally shifting your attention to the positive, creating a balance between the good and the bad. Think of it like a mental muscle that you strengthen with consistent practice. As you cultivate this gratitude muscle, it becomes easier to notice and appreciate the small joys that often slip by unnoticed in the daily grind.

To begin your gratitude meditation practice, find a quiet place where you can relax and focus without distractions. It can be your bedroom, a park bench, or even a cozy corner in your office. Sit comfortably, close your eyes, and take a few deep breaths, allowing your body to settle into a state of relaxation. As you breathe, visualize yourself surrounded by a soft, warm light that represents peace and gratitude.

Now, start thinking about the things in your life that you are grateful for. It could be something simple like a warm cup of coffee on a cold morning, a beautiful sunrise, or a kind word from a loved one. Allow yourself to dwell on these positive experiences, feeling the warmth of gratitude rise within you. As you explore your feelings of gratitude, you might notice a shift in your perspective. The world around you seems brighter, more vibrant, and filled with possibilities.

Don't feel limited by the big things. Gratitude can be found in the smallest moments. Maybe it's the taste of a delicious meal, the feeling of fresh air on your skin, or the laughter of a child. These small, everyday joys, often overlooked in the busyness of life, become precious treasures when you take the time to acknowledge and appreciate them.

Gratitude meditation can be practiced for as long as you like, starting with a few minutes and gradually extending the time as you become more comfortable. You might find it helpful to keep a gratitude journal where you can write down your thoughts and reflections after each session. This not only strengthens your practice but also provides a written record of your journey of appreciating the good in your life.

Think of it like this: Gratitude is a superpower, a lens through which you can view your life with a fresh perspective, allowing you to see the beauty, joy, and abundance that often go unnoticed. By practicing gratitude meditation regularly, you begin to shift your mindset from scarcity to abundance, from negativity to positivity. This shift not only enhances your happiness and well-being but also empowers you to create a life filled with purpose, joy, and contentment.

Here are some practical tips for practicing gratitude meditation:

- **Choose a specific time:** Make it a part of your daily routine, like first thing in the morning or before bed. Consistency is key.
- **Use a guided meditation:** There are many guided gratitude meditations available online or through meditation apps.
- **Focus on your senses:** Engage your senses to deepen your experience of gratitude. Notice the colors, sounds, smells, and textures around you.
- **Be specific:** Instead of just saying "I'm grateful for my family," think about specific things you are grateful for about them, like their love, support, and laughter.
- **Express your gratitude:** Write a thank-you note, call a loved one, or perform a random act of kindness. These actions solidify your feelings of gratitude and spread joy.

As you practice gratitude meditation, you may notice a shift in your overall perspective. You may find yourself feeling more optimistic, resilient, and joyful. The world around you may seem brighter, more hopeful, and filled with possibilities.

Remember, gratitude is not about pretending that life is perfect. It's about acknowledging the good, even amidst the challenges. It's about finding the silver lining, even when things are tough. And it's about recognizing that you have so much to be thankful for, no matter what life throws your way.

Gratitude meditation is a powerful tool for cultivating happiness, well-being, and a more fulfilling life. It's a simple yet profound practice that can transform your perspective, reminding you of all the amazing things you have to be grateful for. So, take a few moments each day to practice gratitude, and watch as your life unfolds with renewed joy, appreciation, and abundance.

Cultivating a Mindful Lifestyle

Mindfulness, like a gentle breeze, whispers through our daily lives, inviting us to pause, to truly see, and to savor the present moment. It's not about escaping reality; it's about embracing it with an open heart and an awakened mind. Integrating mindfulness into our daily routines can transform our experiences, infusing them with a sense of presence and gratitude.

Imagine yourself sitting down to a meal, not just to fuel your body but to engage all your senses. The vibrant colors of the food, the delicate aromas that tickle your nostrils, the textures that dance on your tongue. Each detail becomes a moment of mindful appreciation. As you savor each bite, you notice the subtle flavors and the satisfying crunch or the velvety smoothness, truly experiencing the food in its entirety. This mindful eating is not about deprivation but about savoring the experience, appreciating the nourishment it brings, and finding joy in the simplest of pleasures.

Mindful movement is another powerful tool for cultivating a mindful lifestyle. Think of walking, not just as a way to get from point A to point B, but as a chance to connect with your body. Notice the rhythm of your steps, the feel of the ground beneath your feet, the gentle sway of your arms. Engage your senses, observe the world around you, and let your mind wander freely, without judgment. Yoga or tai chi, with their emphasis on controlled movements and breathwork, offer a rich avenue for mindful movement, encouraging a deeper connection between body and mind.

The world of communication is often filled with distractions and noise. It's easy to rush through conversations, responding without truly listening, or allowing emotions to cloud our judgment. Mindful communication, however, invites us to engage with others with intention and awareness. It's about listening with an open heart, paying attention to both verbal and non-verbal cues, and responding with empathy and understanding. It's about expressing ourselves with clarity and compassion, choosing our words carefully and considering the impact they may have. Mindful communication is not about perfection, but about creating a space for connection and mutual respect.

Imagine yourself in a conversation with a loved one, fully present and attentive. You notice their body language, their tone of voice, and the emotions that flicker across their face. You listen not just to their words, but to the unspoken messages they convey. You respond thoughtfully, reflecting on their words before offering your own perspective. This mindful approach to communication can strengthen bonds, resolve conflicts constructively, and foster deeper understanding.

Cultivating a mindful lifestyle is a journey, not a destination. It's about embracing the present moment, acknowledging our thoughts and feelings without judgment, and finding joy in the simplest of things. By integrating mindfulness into our daily lives, we can transform our experiences, enhance our well-being, and cultivate a deeper connection with ourselves and the world around us.

Here are some practical tips for integrating mindfulness into your daily routines:

Mindful Eating:

- **Set aside time for your meals:** Avoid rushing through your meals. Sit down at a table, turn off distractions, and allow yourself to fully experience the food.

- **Engage all your senses:** Notice the colors, textures, and aromas of your food. Appreciate the sounds of your chewing and the taste of each bite.

- **Eat slowly and savor each mouthful:** Take small bites and chew slowly, savoring the flavors and textures.

- **Be present with your food:** Avoid distractions like television, phones, or reading. Focus on the act of eating and appreciate the nourishment it provides.

Mindful Movement:

- **Start with simple walks:** Take a mindful walk in nature or around your neighborhood. Notice the feel of the ground beneath your feet, the movement of your body, and the sights and sounds around you.

- **Incorporate yoga or tai chi:** These practices encourage a mindful connection between body and mind.

- **Be present with your exercise:** Whether you're running, swimming, or lifting weights, focus on the sensations of your body and the rhythm of your breath.

Mindful Communication:

- **Practice active listening:** Pay full attention to the person speaking. Engage with their words, observe their body language, and respond thoughtfully.

- **Speak with intention:** Choose your words carefully, considering the impact they may have on the listener. Express yourself clearly and compassionately.

- **Be mindful of your tone of voice:** Avoid speaking in a hurried or dismissive manner. Use a calm and respectful tone.

- **Be present in conversations:** Avoid distractions like phones or other devices. Focus your attention on the person you're speaking with.

Mindful Breathing:

- **Find a quiet spot:** Sit comfortably in a chair or on the floor, with your back straight but not stiff.

- **Focus on your breath:** Notice the natural rhythm of your breath, the rise and fall of your chest and abdomen.

- **Follow your breath:** As you inhale, notice the sensation of air entering your nostrils. As you exhale, notice the sensation of air leaving your body.

- **Be gentle with your mind:** If your mind wanders, gently guide it back to your breath. Don't judge yourself for getting distracted, simply notice the distraction and return to your breath.

Mindful Living:

- **Practice mindfulness in daily activities:** Bring mindfulness to everyday activities like showering, brushing your teeth, or washing dishes. Pay attention to the sensations of your body, the sights and sounds around you, and the emotions that arise.

- **Set aside time for mindfulness:** Schedule regular time for meditation or mindfulness practice. Even a few minutes each day can make a difference.

- **Be patient with yourself:** Mindfulness is a skill that takes practice. Be patient with yourself and don't get discouraged if you find it challenging at first.

As you continue to practice mindfulness, you'll start to notice a shift in your perception of the world. You'll become more aware of your thoughts, feelings, and sensations. You'll develop a deeper appreciation for the beauty of the present moment. And you'll discover a sense of peace and calm that permeates every aspect of your life.

CHAPTER 14

EMBRACING YOUR SPIRITUAL SIDE

The Importance of Spirituality

Our journey of self-discovery has led us to explore various facets of our being, from understanding our emotions to nurturing our physical and mental well-being. Now, we reach a realm often shrouded in mystery yet deeply influential in shaping our lives: spirituality.

Spirituality is not about adhering to a specific religion or dogma; it's a deeply personal journey of seeking meaning, purpose, and connection to something greater than ourselves. It's about exploring the essence of who we are, the source of our existence, and our place in the vast tapestry of life.

For some, spirituality might manifest as a connection to a higher power, a divine presence, or a universal energy. For others, it might be a profound sense of interconnectedness with nature, humanity, or the cosmos. It could be a feeling of awe and wonder, a yearning for something more, or a deep sense of peace and tranquility.

The path to spirituality is as diverse as the individuals who embark upon it. There is no one-size-fits-all approach, no right or wrong way to explore this inner landscape. It's about finding what resonates with you, what sparks your curiosity and ignites a sense of purpose within your heart.

Spirituality can be a source of profound strength and guidance, offering solace in times of adversity, hope in moments of doubt, and a sense of purpose that transcends the limitations of our everyday lives. It can help us find meaning in the face of suffering, connect with a deeper truth beyond the surface of things, and cultivate compassion and love for ourselves and others.

Here are some ways spirituality can enrich our lives:

1. Finding Meaning and Purpose:

The search for meaning is an inherent human need. It's a quest to understand our role in the grand scheme of things, to discover our place in the universe, and to find a reason to get out of bed each morning. Spirituality can offer a framework for answering these existential questions, providing a sense of purpose that guides our actions and infuses our lives with meaning.

Imagine a world where you wake up each day feeling driven by an inner compass, a deep sense of knowing your true purpose. You feel connected to something larger than yourself, something that inspires you to act with courage, compassion, and unwavering dedication. This is the transformative power of finding meaning through spirituality.

2. Cultivating Inner Peace and Joy:

In a world driven by constant demands and expectations, finding inner peace can feel like an elusive dream. But spirituality offers a path to serenity, a sanctuary where we can quiet our busy minds, connect with our inner selves, and experience a deep sense of peace and joy.

Imagine a place within you where you can access calmness, serenity, and a sense of connection to something greater than yourself. This is the power of meditation, prayer, or other spiritual practices. These practices can help us still the endless chatter of our minds, releasing negative thoughts and anxieties, allowing us to experience a state of tranquility and joy that transcends the ups and downs of daily life.

3. Developing Compassion and Empathy:

Spirituality often emphasizes the interconnectedness of all living beings. It teaches us that we are all part of a larger web of life, intricately connected through an unseen energy or force. This understanding can cultivate compassion and empathy, helping us see the world from the perspective of others, recognizing our shared humanity and the importance of treating each other with kindness and respect.

Imagine a world where you extend kindness to everyone you encounter, where you see the light within each person, and where you understand that we are all connected in ways we may not always see. This is the power of compassion cultivated through spirituality.

4. Overcoming Challenges and Adversity:

Life inevitably throws challenges our way. But when we have a strong spiritual foundation, we can navigate these difficult times with greater resilience, strength, and hope. Spirituality provides a source of comfort, guidance, and support, reminding us that we are not alone, that there is something bigger than our own challenges, and that we have the inner strength to overcome adversity.

Imagine a world where you face challenges with courage and determination, where you find solace in moments of hardship, and where you draw upon a deeper source of strength within. This is the power of resilience cultivated through spirituality.

5. Connecting with Something Greater:

Spirituality often involves seeking a connection to something beyond ourselves, a force or energy that transcends the limitations of our physical world. This connection can provide a sense of belonging, purpose, and meaning, reminding us that we are part of something larger than ourselves, something that inspires awe and wonder.

Imagine a world where you feel connected to a vast source of energy, a universal intelligence, or a higher power. This is the power of finding connection through spirituality, a sense of unity that transcends boundaries and connects us to the boundless possibilities of the universe.

Embracing our spiritual side is an invitation to explore the depths of our being, to discover the source of our true selves, and to connect with a greater sense of purpose and meaning. It is a journey of self-discovery, self-acceptance, and self-transcendence, a path that can lead us to a life filled with joy, peace, and profound fulfillment.

As we explore this path, let us remember that there is no right or wrong way to be spiritual. The journey is unique to each individual, shaped by our own experiences, beliefs, and aspirations. Let us approach this exploration with an open heart, a curious mind, and a willingness to embrace the infinite possibilities that lie within our own spiritual depths.

Finding Your Spiritual Path

The journey to find your spiritual path can feel like embarking on an ancient pilgrimage, a quest for a hidden treasure within your own being. It's not about adhering to a specific dogma or blindly following a set of rules. It's about discovering a connection to something larger than yourself, something that resonates with your deepest values and beliefs, which fuels your soul and gives your life meaning.

The first step on this path is to open your mind and your heart to possibilities. Explore different spiritual traditions and practices with an open and curious spirit, allowing yourself to be guided by your intuition. From the ancient wisdom of Eastern philosophies to the contemplative practices of Christianity, Judaism, or Islam, or perhaps even exploring the power of nature through paganism or shamanism, the world of spirituality offers a diverse tapestry of paths. Each path, like a thread in this tapestry, can lead you to a deeper understanding of yourself and the universe. Don't be afraid to try different practices, to experiment with meditation, yoga, prayer, or simply spending time in nature. You might find that one practice resonates with you more than another, or that a combination of different practices provides the perfect blend for your spiritual journey.

As you explore these different traditions, pay attention to your inner compass. What feels true to you? What sparks a sense of resonance within your soul? Remember, there is no single right path. It's not about finding the "perfect" religion or practice but rather discovering the one that speaks to your heart and aligns with your core values. Trust your intuition, your inner voice, and allow it to guide you towards the path that feels most authentic and fulfilling.

Imagine a tapestry woven with threads of different colors and textures. Each thread represents a unique spiritual practice or tradition, each offering its own unique perspective and wisdom. Some threads may be bold and vibrant, while others may be delicate and subtle. Some may draw you in with their intricate patterns, while others may captivate you with their simplicity. As you explore this tapestry, you'll discover which threads resonate with you, which ones feel like a natural extension of your own inner wisdom.

Take the time to read sacred texts from various traditions, learn about different spiritual leaders and their teachings, and immerse yourself in the practices that call to you. You might find yourself drawn to the ancient wisdom of the Upanishads, the contemplative teachings of the Buddha, or the inspiring stories of the Bible. Don't be afraid to experiment, to ask questions, and to challenge your own beliefs. The more you explore, the more you'll discover what truly resonates with you.

Perhaps you'll find solace in the quiet contemplation of nature, feeling a sense of awe and connection to the universe as you witness the beauty of a sunrise or the intricate dance of leaves in the wind. Or maybe you'll find inspiration in the stories of saints, prophets, or spiritual teachers who have walked a similar path before you, their words echoing with profound wisdom and guidance.

As you explore deeper into spirituality, you may discover that it's not just about a set of practices or beliefs, but a way of life. It's about living with intention, with compassion, with a sense of gratitude for the beauty and wonder of life. It's about connecting with your inner self, discovering your true nature, and aligning your thoughts, words, and actions with your deepest values.

Your spiritual journey may not be linear or straightforward. There will be times of doubt, of questioning, and of seeking. But remember, the process itself is a journey of growth, of self-discovery, of connecting with a deeper sense of meaning and purpose. Embrace the challenges, the setbacks, and the moments of uncertainty, for they are all part of the process that leads you closer to your spiritual truth.

Think of it like exploring a vast and beautiful forest. You might stumble upon a hidden path, a secluded grove, or a breathtaking vista that takes your breath away. And just as a forest is full of different trees, plants, and creatures, each unique and essential to the ecosystem, so too is the spiritual world a tapestry of diverse traditions and practices, each offering its own unique beauty and wisdom. Explore with an open mind, a curious spirit, and an open heart. You never know what treasures you might discover on your spiritual journey.

Some may find solace in prayer, finding comfort in connecting with a higher power through words and contemplation. Others may find solace in meditation, quieting the mind and connecting with their inner selves through focused breathing and mindfulness. Still, others may find spiritual fulfillment through acts of service, extending kindness and compassion to those in need.

There is no one-size-fits-all approach to finding your spiritual path. The journey is unique to each individual, a personal exploration of the deepest aspects of your being. Embrace the journey with open arms, allowing yourself to be guided by your intuition, your values, and your inner wisdom. The treasures you discover along the way will be worth more than you can imagine.

Think of your spiritual path as a compass, guiding you towards a deeper understanding of yourself and your place in the universe. It's a journey of self-discovery, a quest for meaning and purpose, and a connection to something larger than yourself. It's a journey worth embarking on, a journey that can transform your life and lead you towards a life filled with greater joy, peace, and fulfillment.

As you embark on this journey, remember that you are not alone. There are countless others who have walked this path before you, leaving behind a legacy of wisdom, inspiration, and guidance. Reach out to spiritual teachers, mentors, or fellow seekers, sharing your experiences and seeking their insights. And remember, the most important guide on this journey is your own inner wisdom. Trust your intuition, listen to your heart, and allow it to guide you towards the path that feels most authentic and fulfilling.

The journey to find your spiritual path can be a lifelong exploration, a continuous process of growth and discovery. Embrace the journey, learn from your experiences, and never stop seeking a deeper understanding of yourself and the universe. The rewards of this journey are immeasurable, leading to a life filled with greater meaning, purpose, and joy.

The Power of Prayer and Reflection

The human spirit, in its infinite wisdom, has long recognized the profound connection between our inner selves and the unseen forces that govern our existence. From ancient rituals to modern-day practices, humanity has sought ways to transcend the physical realm and tap into a higher consciousness. This pursuit, often referred to as spirituality, encompasses a wide spectrum of beliefs, practices, and experiences, all of which aim to foster a sense of meaning, purpose, and connection.

Prayer, in its essence, is a form of communication with the divine, a heartfelt outpouring of our desires, hopes, and fears. It can be a solitary act of reflection, a shared moment of communion, or a whispered plea for guidance. Regardless of its form, prayer acts as a bridge between our earthly existence and a realm of infinite possibilities. When we pray, we open ourselves to a source of strength, wisdom, and love that transcends our limited understanding.

Imagine a bustling city street, filled with the cacophony of honking cars, chattering crowds, and the constant hum of activity. In this midst of chaos, a lone individual finds solace in a small, quiet park. They sit on a bench, closing their eyes and taking deep breaths. The world around them fades away, replaced by a sense of inner peace and tranquility. This is the power of reflection, the ability to step away from the noise and distractions of daily life and connect with our inner selves.

Through prayer and reflection, we create a sacred space within ourselves, a sanctuary where we can quiet the incessant chatter of our minds and listen to the whispers of our souls. These practices allow us to tap into a wellspring of wisdom and intuition that lies dormant within us, waiting to be discovered.

Prayer and reflection are not merely passive activities; they are active engagements with our inner selves. They require intention, focus, and a willingness to let go of our preconceived notions and embrace the unknown.

When we pray, we are not simply asking for something; we are opening ourselves to the possibility of receiving something greater than we can imagine. When we reflect, we are not simply pondering our thoughts; we are engaging in a deep and profound conversation with our souls.

The benefits of prayer and reflection are as vast as the human spirit itself. These practices have been shown to reduce stress and anxiety, promote emotional well-being, enhance creativity, and foster a sense of purpose and meaning in life. They can help us to connect with our inner wisdom, develop compassion for ourselves and others, and cultivate a deeper understanding of our place in the universe.

Prayer: A Bridge to the Divine

Prayer, in its many forms, is a universal practice that transcends cultural boundaries. It is a way of connecting with a higher power, a source of strength, wisdom, and love that exists beyond our earthly limitations. The act of prayer can be as simple as a silent moment of contemplation or as elaborate as a formal ritual involving chants, incense, and sacred objects.

The beauty of prayer lies in its inherent personalization. It is a dialogue between our individual selves and the divine, a space where we can express our deepest desires, fears, and aspirations. We can pray for guidance, strength, healing, or simply for a moment of peace.

Prayer can be a powerful tool for transformation. It can help us to release negative emotions, cultivate a sense of gratitude, and connect with our inner wisdom. It can provide a sense of comfort and support during difficult times, reminding us that we are not alone in our struggles.

The Power of Reflection

Reflection, in its purest form, is a journey inward, a process of introspection that allows us to examine our thoughts, feelings, and experiences with a discerning mind. It is a space where we can cultivate self-awareness, gain clarity, and deepen our understanding of ourselves and the world around us.

Reflection can take many forms, from journaling to meditation to simply taking a walk in nature and observing the world around us. The key is to create a space where we can quiet the noise of our minds and connect with our inner selves.

Practical Tips for Prayer and Reflection

- **Find a quiet space:** Seek out a place where you can be alone and undisturbed. This could be a quiet corner of your home, a peaceful park, or a secluded spot in nature.

- **Set aside time:** Dedicate a specific amount of time each day for prayer or reflection. Even a few minutes can make a difference.

- **Be intentional:** Approach prayer and reflection with an open heart and a sincere desire to connect with something greater than yourself.

- **Listen to your intuition:** Pay attention to the thoughts, feelings, and insights that arise during your practice.

- **Be patient:** The benefits of prayer and reflection may not be immediate, but with consistent practice, you will begin to experience the profound impact these practices can have on your life.

Exploring Different Spiritual Practices

The journey of exploring your spiritual side is a deeply personal one. There are countless spiritual practices and traditions available, each with its own unique set of beliefs and practices. Some popular practices include:

- **Meditation:** Meditation is a practice of focusing the mind on a single point, such as a mantra or your breath. It can help to reduce stress, improve concentration, and cultivate a sense of inner peace.

- **Yoga:** Yoga is a combination of physical postures, breathing techniques, and meditation. It can improve flexibility, strength, and balance, as well as promote emotional well-being.

- **Mindfulness:** Mindfulness is a practice of paying attention to the present moment without judgment. It can help to reduce stress, improve focus, and cultivate a sense of self-awareness.

- **Energy healing:** Energy healing practices, such as Reiki and qigong, involve channeling energy to promote healing and balance.

Embracing Your Spiritual Journey

Exploring your spiritual side is not about finding the "right" path or subscribing to a particular set of beliefs. It is about discovering what resonates with your soul, what brings you a sense of peace, purpose, and connection. It is a journey of self-discovery, a process of seeking deeper meaning and understanding in your life.

Be open to exploring different practices and traditions. Listen to your intuition. And remember, the journey is just as important as the destination. As you embark on this journey, be patient with yourself, embrace the unknown, and trust in the power of your own inner wisdom.

The human spirit is a complex and multifaceted entity, capable of great depths of love, compassion, and understanding. By embracing our spiritual side, we tap into a wellspring of potential, opening ourselves to a world of infinite possibilities. Prayer and reflection are powerful tools that can guide us on this journey, providing solace, wisdom, and a sense of connection that transcends the limitations of our physical existence.

Through these practices, we can cultivate inner peace, deepen our self-awareness, and foster a sense of gratitude and purpose in our lives. Embrace the transformative power of prayer and reflection, and allow them to guide you towards a more fulfilling and meaningful life.

The Role of Forgiveness and Compassion

Forgiveness is not about condoning the actions of others; it is about releasing yourself from the shackles of bitterness, resentment, and anger that hold you captive. It is a powerful act of self-love, a conscious decision to break free from the chains of the past and embrace the healing power of letting go.

Imagine carrying a heavy weight on your shoulders, a burden of pain and negativity that weighs you down. This weight is the result of past hurts, betrayals, and injustices that have left scars on your soul. You may have tried to ignore it, suppress it, or even lash out in anger, but the weight remains, a constant reminder of the pain that you have endured.

Forgiveness offers a path to liberation from this heavy burden. It is not about forgetting what happened or minimizing the pain you experienced. Rather, it is about choosing to move beyond the hurt and embrace a sense of inner peace. When you forgive, you are not saying that what happened was okay. You are simply choosing to release the hold that the past has on your present and future.

Forgiveness is a journey, not a destination. It may not happen overnight, and it may require time, effort, and even a willingness to confront painful emotions. However, the rewards of forgiveness are immeasurable. It can lead to:

- **Reduced stress and anxiety:** Holding onto anger and resentment creates a constant state of stress and anxiety that can affect your physical and mental well-being. Forgiveness helps to release this negativity, allowing you to experience a sense of peace and tranquility.

- **Improved relationships:** Forgiveness can mend broken relationships and create a foundation for healthier, more fulfilling connections. It can help you to move past conflicts and build bridges of understanding with those who have hurt you.

- **Increased happiness and well-being:** When you are free from the weight of bitterness and resentment, you are able to experience more joy, happiness, and fulfillment in your life. Forgiveness allows you to embrace the present moment with a lighter heart and a more positive outlook.

- **Enhanced self-compassion:** Forgiveness requires a deep level of self-compassion. You must be willing to acknowledge your own pain and forgive yourself for any role you may have played in the situation. This act of self-forgiveness can lead to greater self-love and acceptance.

- **Spiritual growth:** Forgiveness is an essential aspect of spiritual growth. It allows you to connect with a higher power, transcend the limitations of the ego, and experience a sense of inner peace and unity.

Forgiveness is not just about letting go of negativity; it is also about embracing compassion. When you forgive, you choose to see the humanity in the person who has hurt you, even if their actions were hurtful or wrong. You acknowledge that everyone makes mistakes, and that everyone is capable of growth and change.

Compassion is the ability to understand and share the suffering of others. It is a quality that can help us to connect with others on a deeper level and to extend forgiveness more easily. When we cultivate compassion, we are less likely to judge others and more likely to offer understanding and forgiveness.

Forgiveness and compassion are powerful tools for healing and transformation. They can help us to release the negativity of the past and create space for peace, joy, and love in our lives. By embracing forgiveness and compassion, we can unlock our spiritual potential and live a life of greater meaning and fulfillment.

Here are some practical tips for practicing forgiveness:

- **Acknowledge your pain:** Before you can forgive, you must acknowledge the pain you have experienced. Allow yourself to feel the emotions, without judgment, and allow yourself to grieve the loss of what was.

- **Write a forgiveness letter:** Write a letter to the person you are struggling to forgive. Express your hurt and anger, but also express your desire for healing and peace. You may choose to send the letter or keep it for yourself.

- **Practice self-compassion:** Be kind to yourself during this process. Remember that you are human and you are not alone in experiencing pain.

- **Focus on the present moment:** Instead of dwelling on the past, focus your attention on the present moment. Engage in activities that bring you joy and help you to feel grounded.

- **Seek support:** Talk to a trusted friend, family member, therapist, or spiritual advisor. Sharing your pain and seeking support can help you to process your emotions and move forward.

Remember, forgiveness is a process, not an event. It may take time, and you may experience setbacks along the way. Be patient with yourself and continue to work on releasing the negativity that is holding you back.

Forgiveness is not a sign of weakness; it is a sign of strength. It is a testament to your willingness to let go of the past and embrace a brighter future. By choosing to forgive, you choose to heal your heart, liberate your spirit, and create a more peaceful and joyful life.

Living a Life of Service

Living a life of service is a profound and transformative experience that can profoundly enrich our lives and connect us to something greater than ourselves. It is a journey of compassion, empathy, and selfless giving that has the power to uplift not only those we help but also our own spirits.

Imagine a world where everyone felt a deep sense of purpose and responsibility to make a positive difference in the lives of others. Imagine the collective power we could unleash if we all embraced the opportunity to serve and contribute our unique gifts and talents to the well-being of our communities. This is the vision of a life of service – a life that transcends the boundaries of self-interest and embraces the interconnectedness of all beings.

The spiritual rewards of living a life of service are immeasurable. When we step outside ourselves and focus on the needs of others, we tap into a wellspring of love, compassion, and gratitude that can elevate our consciousness and bring a sense of fulfillment that goes far beyond material possessions or personal achievements.

Here are some ways you can live a life of service:

- **Volunteer your time:** Whether it's at a local soup kitchen, an animal shelter, or a community garden, there are countless opportunities to give back to your community. Volunteering allows you to connect with others, make a tangible difference in the lives of those in need, and gain a sense of purpose and fulfillment.

- **Donate to charities:** Supporting organizations that are working to address important social issues, such as poverty, hunger, or environmental protection, can have a profound impact. Your financial contributions can provide essential resources and support to those who need it most.

- **Mentor others:** Sharing your knowledge, skills, and experience with others can be incredibly rewarding. Mentoring can help you grow as a leader, develop your communication skills, and make a lasting impact on the lives of those you guide.

- **Be kind and compassionate:** Small acts of kindness can have a ripple effect, spreading positivity and joy to those around you. Hold a door open for someone, offer a helping hand, or simply listen with empathy and understanding.

- **Practice gratitude:** Cultivating a grateful heart can open your eyes to the blessings in your life and inspire you to share your good fortune with others. Express your gratitude to those who have helped you, and find ways to give back to those in need.

- **Live with intention:** Every day presents an opportunity to live a life of purpose and service. Make a conscious effort to be mindful of your actions and consider how you can make a positive difference in the world.

Remember that living a life of service is not about seeking recognition or reward; it is about embracing the inherent goodness within ourselves and sharing it with the world. When we choose to serve others, we not only make a positive impact on their lives, but we also transform our own hearts and minds, cultivating a deeper sense of purpose, compassion, and joy.

Living a life of service is a journey of continuous learning and growth. As we open our hearts to the needs of others, we discover a wellspring of empathy, resilience, and kindness within ourselves. We learn to appreciate the interconnectedness of all beings and the profound impact our actions have on the world. This journey of service is a testament to the human spirit's capacity for compassion, generosity, and love – qualities that have the power to transform both our individual lives and the world around us.

CHAPTER 15

THE JOURNEY CONTINUES: EMBRACING A LIFE OF PURPOSE AND FULFILLMENT

Reflecting on Your Growth

As you stand at the precipice of this new chapter, the one you've meticulously crafted through your self-discovery journey, take a moment to bask in the warmth of your accomplishments. Look back on the path you've traversed, not with a focus on the stumbles or setbacks, but with a heart brimming with gratitude for the lessons learned and the wisdom gained.

Remember the first steps when you might have felt lost, adrift in a sea of uncertainties. Perhaps you were grappling with self-doubt, struggling to define your worth or uncover your hidden talents. Maybe you were consumed by a relentless inner critic, a voice that whispered negativity and kept you bound by fear.

But you pressed on, didn't you? You dared to venture into the depths of your being, to confront your fears, and to embrace the unknown. You picked up the tools of self-awareness, tools that allowed you to see yourself with greater clarity, to identify your core values, and to understand the intricate workings of your thoughts and emotions.

Through introspection, you began to unravel the intricate tapestry of your being. You unearthed your passions, the embers of desire that had long been dormant within. You recognized your strengths, the unique gifts that set you apart. And with each revelation, your sense of self-worth grew stronger, your confidence blossomed, and your belief in your own potential took root.

Recall the pivotal moments, the turning points that marked your progress. Maybe it was the day you finally silenced the negative voice, replacing it with a chorus of self-compassion and encouragement. Perhaps it was the moment you decided to break free from limiting beliefs, to challenge the narratives that had held you captive for far too long.

Perhaps it was the day you took a leap of faith, stepping outside of your comfort zone and embracing a new challenge. Maybe it was the discovery of a new passion, a pursuit that ignited your soul and filled your days with purpose and meaning.

Each of these moments, each step forward, was a testament to your unwavering commitment to personal growth. It was proof that you were not only willing to change, but you were capable of achieving remarkable transformations.

As you reflect on your journey, acknowledge the lessons learned along the way. The challenges you faced, the mistakes you made, the triumphs you celebrated – they are all interwoven threads in the fabric of your becoming. They have shaped you, molded you, and propelled you forward on your path.

Perhaps you've learned the power of setting boundaries, of saying no when necessary, and of prioritizing your own well-being. Maybe you've discovered the transformative power of gratitude, the simple act of appreciating the beauty and blessings that surround you.

You might have unearthed the importance of vulnerability, the courage to let down your guard and connect with others on a deeper level. Or perhaps you've learned the art of forgiveness, both for yourself and for others, a practice that releases negativity and opens the door to inner peace.

Remember, self-discovery is not a linear journey. It is a winding, sometimes unpredictable path, filled with twists and turns. There will be moments of triumph and moments of doubt, times when you feel like you are making great strides and times when you feel stuck or overwhelmed. But it is the unwavering commitment to your own growth, the willingness to learn and evolve, that truly defines your journey.

So, as you look back on the road traveled, recognize the strength you've cultivated, the resilience you've honed, and the wisdom you've gained. Celebrate your progress, not with arrogance, but with a heart full of gratitude for the individual you are becoming.

And as you step into the uncharted territory of your future, carry with you the lessons learned, the insights gained, and the unwavering belief in your own potential. Embrace the challenges that lie ahead as opportunities for continued growth, knowing that you have the strength, the wisdom, and the courage to navigate any obstacle.

For you are not simply a passenger on this journey. You are the architect of your life, the sculptor of your destiny. The path you walk is yours to define, yours to shape, yours to mold. And with each step you take, you create a life filled with purpose, meaning, and joy.

Embracing the Power of Now

The present moment is a gift, a precious and fleeting opportunity to experience the fullness of life. Yet, in our fast-paced world, we often get caught up in the whirlwind of our thoughts, worries, and anxieties, missing the beauty and joy that surrounds us. We dwell on the past, regretting missed opportunities or clinging to past hurts, or we anxiously project ourselves into the future, fretting about what might or might not happen. In doing so, we lose sight of the only moment that truly matters, the now.

Imagine yourself walking along a picturesque path, surrounded by vibrant wildflowers and the sweet scent of blooming honeysuckle. You're captivated by the stunning scenery, but as you take a step, your mind starts to wander. You begin thinking about the unfinished tasks waiting for you at home, or the upcoming meeting you're feeling anxious about. In that moment, the beauty of the present disappears, overshadowed by the worries and anxieties that clutter your mind.

This tendency to lose ourselves in our thoughts is a common human experience. Our minds are constantly racing, jumping from one thought to another, creating a never-ending internal dialogue. We become so consumed by our thoughts that we fail to truly appreciate the world around us. We miss the subtle nuances of a sunrise, the warmth of a hug, or the genuine laughter of a loved one.

The practice of embracing the power of now is a conscious decision to shift our focus from the past and future to the present moment. It's about recognizing that the only time we truly have control is right now. By cultivating an awareness of the present, we can begin to appreciate the beauty and joy that exists in everyday life, even amidst the challenges and uncertainties that we face.

The Benefits of Embracing the Power of Now

Embracing the present moment offers numerous benefits for our physical, mental, and emotional well-being. It allows us to:

- **Reduce stress and anxiety:** When we're constantly dwelling on the past or worrying about the future, our stress levels increase. Focusing on the present moment helps to calm our minds and reduce anxiety by grounding us in the here and now.

- **Enhance happiness and well-being:** By appreciating the simple pleasures of the present, we cultivate a sense of gratitude and contentment, leading to greater happiness and well-being.

- **Improve focus and concentration:** When our minds are constantly racing, it becomes difficult to focus on tasks at hand. By practicing mindfulness, we train our minds to be present and attentive, improving our ability to focus and concentrate.

- **Increase self-awareness:** Being present in the moment allows us to become more aware of our thoughts, feelings, and sensations. This increased self-awareness helps us to understand ourselves better and make more informed decisions.

- **Strengthen relationships:** When we are truly present with loved ones, we can connect with them on a deeper level, fostering stronger and more meaningful relationships.

Practical Tips for Embracing the Power of Now

Here are some practical tips for incorporating the power of now into your daily life:

- **Practice mindfulness meditation:** Mindfulness meditation involves paying attention to the present moment without judgment. You can start with just five minutes a day, focusing on your breath or the sensations in your body.

- **Engage in mindful activities:** Choose activities that allow you to be fully present, such as walking in nature, listening to music, or enjoying a cup of tea.

- **Notice your thoughts and feelings:** Become aware of the thoughts that run through your mind and the emotions that arise within you. Acknowledge them without judgment and allow them to pass through you.

- **Focus on your senses:** Pay attention to your senses: sight, sound, smell, taste, and touch. Notice the colors, sounds, and textures of your surroundings.

- **Practice gratitude:** Take time each day to appreciate the good things in your life, no matter how small. This can be as simple as being grateful for the warmth of the sun on your skin or the taste of a delicious meal.

- **Disconnect from technology:** Regularly unplug from your devices and social media to give yourself a break from the constant stimulation and distractions of the digital world.

Integrating the Power of Now into Your Daily Routine

The practice of embracing the power of now is not about escaping from reality or ignoring your responsibilities. It's about finding ways to be more present in your daily life, even during routine activities. Here are some ideas:

- **Mindful eating:** Pay attention to the taste, texture, and aroma of your food. Savor each bite and appreciate the experience.

- **Mindful walking:** Notice the sensations of your feet on the ground, the rhythm of your breath, and the sights and sounds around you.

- **Mindful showering:** Focus on the sensations of the water on your skin and the aroma of your soap.

- **Mindful driving:** Avoid distractions and be fully present while driving, paying attention to the road and your surroundings.

- **Mindful conversations:** Be present in your conversations, listening attentively and engaging with the other person on a deeper level.

Embracing the Power of Now: A Journey of Transformation

Embracing the power of now is an ongoing journey, not a destination. It requires continuous practice and a willingness to be present in each moment. As you cultivate awareness of the present, you'll begin to notice a shift in your perception of the world. You'll find yourself appreciating the beauty and joy that surrounds you, even amidst the challenges and uncertainties of life.

Remember, the present moment is all we have. By choosing to be present, we can create a life filled with meaning, joy, and fulfillment. Let go of the past, let go of the future, and embrace the power of now. It's the only moment that truly matters.

Creating a Life You Love

The journey of self-discovery and personal growth is an ongoing adventure, and as you reach this point, you've gained invaluable insights and tools to create a life you truly love. Now, it's time to take those learnings and apply them to the everyday tapestry of your existence. You've invested time and energy in understanding your authentic self, cultivating a positive mindset, mastering your emotions, and nurturing your well-being. You've embraced the power of self-care, strengthened your relationships, overcome obstacles, and discovered your purpose. You've unleashed your creativity, built a life of success, and navigated the ebb and flow of change. You've explored the depths of connection and community, embraced the practice of mindfulness and meditation, and connected with your spiritual side.

This journey isn't about reaching a final destination; it's about the continuous process of becoming. The magic lies in the ongoing evolution, in the constant refinement of your inner compass and the persistent pursuit of a life filled with meaning and joy. As you move forward, remember that the power to create the life you desire rests within you. You've learned to identify and embrace your authentic self, and now it's time to let that truth shine brightly in every facet of your existence.

Imagine a life where you wake up each morning filled with a sense of purpose, a deep knowing that you are living in alignment with your core values and passions. A life where challenges are embraced as opportunities for growth and where setbacks are viewed as stepping stones on the path to success. A life where your relationships are nurtured with authenticity and where your creativity flows freely, bringing you joy and fulfillment. This is the life you are capable of creating, a life that reflects the best version of you.

But building such a life requires continuous effort and commitment. It's about weaving your newfound insights and practices into the fabric of your daily routines. It's about setting goals that are aligned with your vision and consistently taking steps towards achieving them. It's about nurturing your relationships with intention and embracing challenges with resilience and optimism.

Think of it as a garden you tend with love and care. You've cultivated the fertile soil of self-awareness, planted the seeds of positive thinking, and watered the roots of self-compassion. Now, you must continue to nurture the growth, to prune away negative patterns, and to provide the nourishment needed for your dreams to blossom.

This is where the true magic happens. It's not about achieving a perfect life; it's about embracing the imperfections and cherishing the journey. It's about learning to love yourself, to celebrate your strengths, and to embrace your vulnerabilities. It's about finding joy in the simple moments, in the laughter with loved ones, in the quiet moments of reflection, and in the pursuit of your passions.

As you continue to evolve, you'll find that the world around you also begins to shift and change. Your energy, your authenticity, and your unwavering commitment to living a fulfilling life will inspire others to do the same. You will become a beacon of light, radiating the warmth of your own self-love and illuminating the path for those around you.

Remember, there is no finish line. The journey of personal growth is an ongoing adventure. It's about continually learning, growing, and evolving, about becoming the best version of yourself. Embrace the process, celebrate your victories, learn from your setbacks, and never stop seeking the joy and fulfillment that life has to offer. You are capable of creating a life you love, and the world is waiting to see what you will achieve.

This is not a destination, but a path. And you are the only one who can walk it. So, take a deep breath, trust your inner guidance, and step confidently into the future you have dreamed of. The world is your canvas, and your life is the masterpiece you are creating.

The Power of Continued Growth

The journey of self-discovery and personal growth is a lifelong endeavor. It's not a destination to be reached but a continuous path we traverse, constantly evolving and becoming the best versions of ourselves. Just like a river that flows endlessly, our journey of self-improvement never truly ends.

Imagine a magnificent oak tree that stands tall and strong, its roots deeply embedded in the earth, and its branches reaching towards the sky. The oak has grown over decades, weathering storms and enduring harsh conditions. Yet, even in its maturity, the oak continues to grow, adapting to changing seasons and embracing the cycle of life.

Similarly, our journey of self-growth is a continuous process of learning, evolving, and adapting. It's not about achieving perfection; it's about embracing our imperfections and striving to become the best versions of ourselves.

Think about the times in your life when you've learned something new or overcome a challenge. These experiences have helped you grow and become stronger. Maybe you've learned a new skill, mastered a difficult task, or navigated a challenging situation. Each experience has left its mark, shaping your character and expanding your capabilities.

The power of continued growth lies in the willingness to step outside our comfort zones, embrace new challenges, and learn from our experiences. It's about being open to feedback, seeking out new knowledge, and remaining curious about the world around us.

Just as the oak tree continues to grow and adapt, we too can cultivate an attitude of continuous learning and improvement. Here are some practical tips to help you embrace the power of continued growth:

- **Embrace a Growth Mindset:** Cultivate a belief that you can always learn and improve. Embrace challenges as opportunities for growth and learning, rather than threats to your ego.

- **Set Intentional Goals:** Establish clear goals that align with your values and aspirations. Having goals gives you a sense of direction and purpose, guiding you towards personal growth and fulfillment.

- **Seek Out New Experiences:** Step outside your comfort zone and embrace new experiences. Explore different hobbies, travel to new places, or try new things.

- **Learn from Your Mistakes:** Embrace failures as opportunities for learning and growth. Analyze your mistakes, identify areas for improvement, and use them as fuel for future success.

- **Reflect Regularly:** Take time to reflect on your experiences, both positive and negative. Journaling, meditation, or simply taking a quiet walk can help you process your thoughts and gain valuable insights.

- **Surround Yourself with Growth-Oriented People:** Connect with individuals who inspire you, challenge you, and support your growth.

- **Embrace Continuous Learning:** Maintain a thirst for knowledge and stay curious. Read books, attend workshops, take online courses, or listen to podcasts that expand your horizons.

The journey of personal growth is a lifelong adventure. It's a journey of discovery, self-improvement, and becoming the best versions of ourselves. By embracing the power of continued growth, we can unlock our full potential and create a life filled with purpose, joy, and fulfillment.

Living a Life Filled with Purpose and Joy

Imagine yourself standing at the precipice of a breathtaking vista, the wind whispering secrets in your ear, the sun painting the sky with hues of gold and crimson. This is the feeling of living a life filled with purpose and joy – a life where every sunrise is a new adventure and every breath is a symphony of gratitude. You are not merely existing; you are thriving, embracing the magnificent tapestry of existence with open arms.

This is not a destination to be reached; it is a journey to be embarked upon. It is a continuous dance of self-discovery, a symphony of personal growth, and a celebration of the extraordinary human spirit. The path may be winding, the terrain challenging, but the rewards are immeasurable.

You are not defined by your past, your failures, or the limitations others might impose on you. You are a masterpiece in progress, a canvas waiting to be filled with the vibrant colors of your dreams and aspirations. Your purpose is not a fixed entity; it is a dynamic force that evolves alongside you, a beacon guiding you toward a life that ignites your soul and sets your spirit soaring.

Perhaps you have always harbored a passion for art, a desire to write, or a yearning to travel the world. Or maybe you feel drawn to making a difference, to leaving a positive mark on the world. These whispers of your heart, these intuitions that tug at your soul, are the threads of your purpose.

The journey begins with a simple act of faith – a faith in yourself, in your potential, and in the power of your own dreams. It is about aligning your actions with your values, your passions, and your desires. It is about embracing the journey, the triumphs, and the challenges, knowing that every step forward is a testament to your strength and resilience.

This is not about achieving a perfect life; it is about creating a life that resonates with your soul, a life that is authentic, meaningful, and joy filled.

Imagine a life where you wake up each morning filled with anticipation, eager to embrace the day's possibilities. Imagine a life where you are surrounded by people who inspire you, support you, and celebrate your journey. Imagine a life where your work aligns with your passions, where every task is a testament to your contribution, and where every accomplishment fuels your soul with fire.

This is the life you are capable of creating. This is the life that awaits you when you choose to live with purpose, joy, and gratitude.

Embrace the adventure. Embrace the journey. Embrace the life that is waiting for you.

APPENDIX

The appendix contains a selection of resources and tools that can support your journey of self-discovery and personal growth. These include:

- **Journaling Prompts**: A series of prompts to help you explore your thoughts, feelings, and aspirations.
- **Self-Reflection Exercises**: Activities to enhance self- awareness, identify your values, and understand your strengths and weaknesses.
- **Affirmation Statements**: Positive affirmations to cultivate a positive mindset and reprogram your subconscious for success.
- **Mindfulness Techniques**: Simple mindfulness exercises to reduce stress, improve focus, and enhance emotional well-being.
- **Recommended Reading List**: A selection of books and articles on personal growth, self-help, and self-discovery.

GLOSSARY

Affirmations: Positive statements that are repeated regularly to reprogram the subconscious mind and create positive beliefs.

Emotional Intelligence (EQ): The ability to understand, manage, and express emotions effectively.

Gratitude: A state of thankfulness and appreciation for the good things in life.

Mindfulness: The practice of paying attention to the present moment without judgment.

Resilience: The ability to bounce back from adversity and overcome challenges.

Self-Awareness: The understanding of one's own thoughts, feelings, and behaviors.

Self-Care: The act of taking care of one's physical, mental, and emotional health.

Values: Core beliefs that guide our actions and decisions.

ABOUT THE AUTHOR

Coach R. LaShun Williams, also known as Rebecca L. Williams, is a powerhouse coach of purpose-driven leadership and transformation. Bringing nearly 30 years of wisdom, heart, and results to everything she touches. Known professionally as Rebecca L. Williams, she has carved a legacy as a sought-after Human Resources consultant, leadership trainer, and empowerment strategist, impacting corporations and individuals around the globe as the founder of **Williams Business Solutions, LLC**, Coach R. LaShun has delivered high-impact HR consulting to international organizations, helping shape strong, values-driven workplaces. She is a **Certified Leadership Trainer and Executive Director with the John Maxwell Team**, as well as a **Professional Certified Coach**, with a gift for helping others unlock their potential and step into the life they were born to lead.

Through her second company, **Your Life Destiny, LLC**, she has guided hundreds of entrepreneurs, teams, and professionals to find clarity, elevate confidence, and achieve success on their own terms. Her influence extends beyond boardrooms and coaching sessions. She has also served as a highly respected youth basketball coach and advocate for over two decades, empowering young girls to rise as confident leaders in sports, school, and life. Coach R. LaShun is the celebrated author of *Throw Like A Girl: How Good Coaches Transform Girls Into Successful Women,* a powerful guide that shows how great mentorship and intentional coaching can build a foundation of lifelong confidence and character.

Rooted in faith, purpose, and a deep commitment to service, Coach R. LaShun's mission is clear: to help others transform their lives and businesses to the level **God desires** for them. She is deeply involved in her community and a passionate youth advocate, channeling her love of family and decades of coaching into empowering the next generation. Known for her authenticity, warmth, and inspirational leadership, she continues to leave an indelible mark on everyone she encounters. She does this one transformed life at a time. Her desires is to guide readers and clients alike to unlock their authentic selves and live with purpose.

Contact Information
Your Life Destiny, LLC
info@yourlifedestiny.com

If you are thinking about starting your Self-Discovery journey:

I AM... (3-Day Challenge):
https://www.yldiam.com/iamchallenge_challenge-page

I AM... (6-Month Journey):
https://www.yldiam.com/iamjourney_journey-page

www.ingramcontent.com/pod-product-compliance
Lightning Source LLC
Chambersburg PA
CBHW061600120626
46550CB00004B/1561
9781967687008